Inspiration For Your Eternal Life

Fifteen Ways To Be Saved

Copyright © 2024 Vincente Garcia

All rights reserved. No portion of this book may be reproduced in any form without written permission from the publisher or author, except as permitted by U.S. copyright law, except for the use of brief quotations in a book review.

Unless otherwise noted, Scripture quotations are taken from the Holy Bible, New International Version, NIV, Zondervan Publishing House, 1984.

ISBN 978-1-954736-34-4 (Paperback)
ISBN 978-1-954736-35-1 (eBook)

Library of Congress Control Number: 2024950591

Authors Inside
P.O. Box 293
Oceano, CA 93475
www.authorsinside.org

Cover design: Laura Gaisie
Editor: Editing by Mel

Printed in the United States of America

I would like to thank Donnie Gooden, George K. L. Smith, and Emmanuel Gaisie for their example of unselfish faith to help others; in the face of utter adversity, they continue to hold open the door for new opportunities for a better life. Without their inspiration this could not have been properly expedited. It's always a pleasure having you all on my side.

Contents

Chapter 1	His Last Hours Begin	1
Chapter 2	The Betrayers Plan Foretold	11
Chapter 3	The New Commandment	21
Chapter 4	Believe and Follow Jesus Christ to God the Father	33
Chapter 5	The Holy Spirit with You forever	47
Chapter 6	Remain in HIS Son Jesus Christ	63
Chapter 7	Jesus Christ our Friend...keep His Commands	81
Chapter 8	The World Hates the Disciples	97
Chapter 9	Holy Spirit will testify...you also must	111
Chapter 10	He did go...He does send	131
Chapter 11	He makes it known	147
Chapter 12	Rejoice in the NAME, Jesus Christ	165
Chapter 13	Take Heart, our Lord Jesus Christ rules, Satan stands condemned	181
Chapter 14	Eternal Life is our God the Father and our Lord Jesus Christ	199
Chapter 15	Unify with our God the Father and our Lord Jesus Christ	217
	About the Author	233

INTRO:

The inspiration for life is found written in these five Chapters, a testimony about our Lord Jesus Christ written by the Apostle John, in Chapters 13 through 17. We will begin to learn the written Word of Truth that was given to us by our living GOD the Father, with HIS testimony that HE spoke through HIS Son, our Lord Jesus Christ.

We are spiritually sanctified by hearing the Word of Truth and the Gospel about our Lord Jesus Christ, then when we are made ready to receive the baptism of the Holy Spirit, as we hear, learn, and believe in the Son of the only living GOD. We must learn to believe and accept our Lord Jesus Christ for salvation and inspiration for our eternal Life.

These messages are written to initiate inspiration as a foundation for those who desire to live their lives righteously and send their love in prayer to those we care for. If only to tell others that we love them and care for them, we are sharing the love of our Lord Jesus Christ with them every day with the power of prayer in spirit for them. We share with others how to live by HIS commands to always love each other in hopes that they will learn enough to do the same to know our GOD the Father and live by HIS testimony. Therefore, we also learn to know the Son of our living GOD. Those who have already been inspired will become stronger in faith when they are reminded how to remain united with the Spirit of our Lord Jesus Christ in themselves.

The five Chapters from the Book of John are divided into fifteen parts, each closing with a daily prayer referencing the message in the scripture of the day for you to learn from and share with others in a fifteen-day cycle. Keep an open mind when you read through these messages as if you are learning the scriptures in the bible for the first time. Take your time to meditate on what is written to let your thoughts, memories, and emotions flow through your heart, mind and soul. You will understand more of what is written in the Word and learn faster, not only about the truth in the Word of GOD but also about yourself and where you are in your life now, compared to who you are supposed to be. That is for you to be inspired with infinite power, love, and self-control to manage your life with direction and purpose.

By the time you complete your first fifteen-day cycle, you may be able to tell the story of your own life in more detail than you ever thought possible as a testimony of your own salvation and inspiration that will make perfect sense of your Life. You may learn that you can be more powerful by having inspiration in yourself, and that you can decide to invoke that power in you at will to help others learn to do the same, especially to glorify our GOD the Father in the name of HIS Son Jesus Christ. You may learn from that one decision how infinitely more powerful you can become by knowing how important you are to so many people, that their lives depend on knowing you and learning the truth about life itself. That decision may prove to be the first and most important decision in your lifetime after you learn how to accept your gift of inspiration for your eternal life in yourself.

Each of the fifteen parts is followed by a (~Notice:), which is an inspired testimony relating to the subjects in the verses that explains how they fit in the Gospel of our Lord Jesus Christ, which is intended to be simple to understand for the first-time reader of the Bible Verses, to help us all reconcile to our GOD the Father. If He did not want us to be completely inspired for our eternal life, he would not have sent our Lord Jesus to sacrifice his life for us to have it in ours.

There are many scriptures, (notes), capitalized words to give emphasis for certain keywords to help support readers to recognize who is speaking to learn faster and have answers to questions that we may think of and may never have asked while reading these scriptures. This is a gift that gives you a way to share our experiences in learning the Word of Truth and the Gospel with family, friends, and others that we meet, to become sanctified in our heart, mind, and soul by the Word of Truth as we are commanded to do by our Lord Jesus Christ, to show that we believe in Him, love Him, and will always love each other.

It is time for you to know our GOD the Father and HIS only begotten Son, our Lord Jesus Christ, by learning to understand how to embrace the inspiration for your eternal life and tap into the gifts that you are destined to have and use to become who you are supposed to be in this life. Those who pray together, stay together. Together we pray in Spirit each day as brothers and sisters all over the world to glorify our GOD the Eternal One, who is calling us to HIMSELF through HIS Son who is our Lord Jesus Christ. Contemplate on the truth written in these Chapters to have inspiration for your eternal life. This is the Word of GOD, and it is the Truth.

Chapter 1: *His Last Hours Begin*

John 13:1-17 NIV

1 It was just before the Passover Festival. Jesus knew that the hour had come for Him to leave this World and go to the Father. Having loved His own who were in the World, He loved them to the end.

2 The (Last Supper) evening meal was in progress, and Satan the devil had already prompted Judas, the son of Simon Iscariot, to betray Jesus.

3 Jesus knew that the Father had put all things under His power and that He had come from GOD and was returning to GOD.

4 So, He got up from the meal, took off His outer clothing, and wrapped a towel around His waist.

5 After that, He poured water into a basin and began to wash His disciples' feet, drying them with the towel that was wrapped around Him.

6 He came to Simon Peter, who said to Him, "Lord, are you going to wash my feet?"

7 Jesus replied, "You do not realize now what I am doing, but later you will understand.

8 No, said Peter, "You shall never wash my feet." Jesus answered, "Unless I wash you, you have no part with Me."

Chapter 1: *His Last Hours Begin*

<u>9</u> Then, Lord," Simon Peter replied, "Not just my feet but my hands and my head as well!"

<u>10</u> Jesus answered, "Those who have had a bath need only to wash their feet; Their whole body is clean. And you are clean, though not every one of you."

<u>11</u> For He knew who was going to betray Him, and that was why He said not everyone was clean.

<u>12</u> When He had finished washing their feet, He put on His clothes and returned to His place. "Do you understand what I have done for you?" He asked them.

<u>13</u> "You call Me 'Teacher' and 'Lord,' and rightly so, for that is what I am.

<u>14</u> Now that I, your Lord, and Teacher, have washed your feet, you also should wash one another's feet.

<u>15</u> I have set you an example that you should do as I have done for you.

<u>16</u> **Very truly I tell you**, no servant is greater than his Master, nor is a messenger greater than the one who sent him.

<u>17</u> Now that you know these things, you will be blessed if you do them".

❖ Notice:

It was time for our Lord Jesus Christ to leave the World and go back to our GOD the Father in Heaven. Yet, His commands, which were given to Him by our GOD the Father were not completed. Because the Apostles were not yet convinced that our Lord Jesus Christ is who He said He is. They still had some spiritual sanctification to do before they all could admit that they believe our Lord Jesus Christ is the Son of our GOD the Father in Heaven, and was sent by our GOD the Father for us to have His Spirit in unity with our personal Spirit for our salvation from sin and death, to share the eternal Life within Him, and for us to have eternal Life within ourselves.

Therefore, our GOD the FATHER gave us HIS Testimony concerning HIS only begotten Son, for us to prove to HIM that we have decided to believe in HIM because we know HIM by what HE has done for Humanity. To enter eternal Life and have our Lord Jesus Christ in unity with you, you must first accept to believe in the Testimony of our living GOD the Father and live by HIS New Covenant.

- **1 John 5:10-11 (NIV)**
  10 Whoever believes in the Son of GOD accepts this Testimony. Whoever does not believe GOD has made HIM out to be a liar, because they have not believed the Testimony GOD has given about HIS Son. **(The Testimony of GOD the Father)** *11 And this is the Testimony: GOD has given us eternal Life, and this Life is in HIS Son. Whoever has the Son has Life; whoever does not have the Son of GOD, does not have Life.*

Our Lord Jesus Christ did not want to leave them in the World before they all believed in Him and the Testimony of GOD the Father with absolute certainty.

Sanctification is the purification of your Body-Temple by the Word of GOD that clears your heart, mind, and soul of any confusion of sinful thoughts and behaviors that lead to living in sin. Knowing the Truth in the Word sets us apart from the World that lives in confusion and lies that cause people to sin. Therefore, we are sanctified by hearing,

Chapter 1: His Last Hours Begin

learning, and believing the Gospel of our Lord Jesus Christ and the message in the Word of Truth. And we remain sanctified as we believe in our Lord Jesus Christ, by doing what the Word of Truth says to do and accepting that our Lord Jesus Christ was sent by our GOD the Father from Heaven to deliver HIS Word of Truth through HIS Son, our Lord Jesus Christ.

The message in the Word of Truth helps us become sanctified to strengthen our faith to believe in our Lord Jesus Christ. It is meant for us to believe and obey the commands in the Word to be saved and stay saved after we receive the Holy Spirit of our GOD the Father and the Spirit of Jesus Christ our Lord to live in complete unity within us. We must learn the Gospel about our Lord Jesus Christ and the message He taught us in the Word by heart, so we may keep His commands, and do what it says at this appointed time on Earth.

When you believe it in your heart and proclaim it with your mouth that "Jesus Christ is your Lord", then at that time you can pray in Spirit to ask of our GOD the Father in the NAME of HIS Son Jesus Christ, to send you HIS Holy Spirit that comes out from our GOD the Father and into you to teach you what you must know to do and say to please our GOD the Father now and for eternal Life.

At that exact time, you will have crossed over from the status of living in death by the desires of the flesh to the status of living with the power of having eternal Life from having HIS Holy Spirit and the Spirit of our Lord Jesus Christ living in complete unity with your Spirit; all within your Body-Temple as One, in complete unity. This is how we have the Spirit of Christ Jesus, the Son of GOD, living within us for eternal Life. And yes, it is time for you to use that guidance to become who you are meant to be with the gifts you will be given to use. Pay attention and be ready at all times to do what you are told to do and say living in Spirit with them.

After you believe in Him and accept to live by the Word of Truth that you learn, you are living in Spirit within our Lord Jesus Christ in unity with your personal Spirit and the Holy Spirit. He is the Church that we live in for those who believe in Him. And you yourself will not be judged or see any shame on the Judgment Day because you have been sanctified by hearing the Word of Truth now, in these scriptures, and are forgiven for your sins that you repented while giving thanks to our GOD the Father, in the NAME of the Son of GOD, Jesus Christ. Now you are living in the Spirit and have our Lord Jesus Christ living in unity with you on Earth for your salvation from the World of corruption until your redemption in Heaven at the Last Day.

You are saved now and marked in our Lord Jesus Christ and hidden in our GOD the Father to be saved now and later to be redeemed as a promise, by HIM sending you HIS Holy Spirit, that you will be redeemed to eternal Life to enter the Kingdom of GOD on that Last Day, the Lords Day. But only those who are saved in our Lord Jesus Christ will live because they have the Word of Truth written in their heart and are marked in our Lord Jesus Christ and living in unity with Him now.

Protect your heart with the written Word that you believe in and know. Keep your heart pure and Holy without sin, so the things you say and do will be without sin, and our Lord Jesus Christ will remain in complete unity within your Body- Temple.

- ### 1 Corinthians 15:33 (NIV)
    33 Do not be misled: "Bad company corrupts good character."

- ### Proverbs 4:23 (NIV)
    23 Above all else, guard your heart, for everything you do flows from it.

- ### Romans 8:8 (NIV)
    8 Therefore, there is now no condemnation for those who are living in Christ Jesus, because through Christ Jesus the (New Covenant) Law of the Spirit who gives Life has set you free from the (Old Covenant) law of sin and death.

Chapter 1: His Last Hours Begin

―――

For what the (Old Covenant) law was powerless to do because it was weakened by the flesh, GOD did, by sending HIS own Son in the likeness of sinful flesh to be a Sin Offering. And so, HE condemned sin in the flesh, in order that the Righteous Requirement of the (New Covenant) Law might be fully met in us, who do not live according to the flesh but live according to the Spirit.

Our Lord Jesus Christ washed the disciple's feet as an example of how much we must care to always love each other; as much as He loves us as Lord of His disciples. He loves us and died for us without sin in Himself to destroy the power of sin in us once and for all who believe in Him so He may live Holy in Spirit within us in complete unity.

Believe in Him and repent your sins so He may forgive you to remove your sin from within you and then live in Spirit as One in you with the power of His eternal Life that He will bestow on your personal Spirit for you to have eternal Life in you. This is how we are anointed with eternal Life, the same way we are anointed and baptized with the Holy Spirit of our GOD the Father in us, we are anointed by THEM both to be living in our Body-Temple with our personal Spirit with which we were formed together with flesh and born with.

Your personal Spirit is in your Body-Temple with the Holy Spirit of our GOD the Father and the Spirit of our Lord Jesus Christ. That is living as One in Spirit in complete unity with them, just as our Lord Jesus Christ had prayed for us to be with THEM as One in Spirit as He is One in Spirit with our GOD the Father.

It was also a lesson to show us that, without His love for us, without accepting His helping us, we cannot be truly sanctified in our Body-Temple to be ready for salvation by the Anointing of our personal Spirit to live in complete unity with THEM. We must continue to contemplate the Word of Truth and keep our minds focused on the things in the Heavenly Realms where we will be taken to live with THEM in the Kingdom of GOD. And if you "reject" the Testimony of our GOD the

INSPIRATION FOR YOUR ETERNAL LIFE

Father concerning HIS Son, and you do not learn to accept to live by the commands in the Word to prove that you love and believe in our Lord Jesus Christ, you will have no part in Him. That means no eternal Life will be in you and you will not have salvation from the Second Death for the destruction of your personal Spirit after you are Judged for your condemnation.

Keep in mind that all the angels that transgressed against the commands of our GOD the Father were cast out of Heaven and hurled down to Earth because they were condemned. And since they turned Humanity into sinners, the entire human race is condemned with them for our transgressions against the Word of Truth. Therefore, the World is corrupted and under the law of death, the wages of sin is death. First your body, then your Spirit in the Second Death.

You will be put to death unless you heed this warning, that you must renounce sin and repent your evil deeds by praying in Spirit while giving thanks to our GOD the Father, in the NAME of HIS Son our Lord Jesus Christ to forgive you. And then ask HIM to send you HIS Holy Spirit to help you learn how to live by HIS Word of Truth. Then practice living by the Testimony of our GOD the Father concerning our Lord Jesus Christ for the inspiration of your eternal Life.

Non-believers are already condemned by their Decision not to have our Lord Jesus Christ living with them, they are Deciding to stay condemned awaiting the Second Death of their Spirit. They will be called up if they are living in the flesh, or if dead even come out from their graves with their sin and evil deeds in them to appear at the Throne of Judgment of our Lord Jesus Christ. They rejected the Holy Spirit and will be there without the Holy Spirit to testify on their behalf. They will appear alone in their personal Spirit with all their evil sin within them standing for condemnation awaiting their doom and destruction.

It is only because they rejected to pray to and live in their Spirit with the Holy Spirit of our GOD the Father, to be living in them and guiding them with the Spirit of our Lord Jesus Christ in their Body-Temple on

Chapter 1: His Last Hours Begin

Earth. Therefore, it may be said, that He never knew them, and they never knew Him by their own Decision not to know Him in this appointed time on Earth to prove how they wished to stand condemned on the Judgement Day. They decided to stay the way they were and stand condemned with sin. And the wages of sin is death by the Second Death of their Spirit. So be it by the Word of Truth they will be terminated the same as the demons will be destroyed for loving sin more than living by the Word of GOD.

The evil of their sin that will be in them, will be used against them when they are raised up to hear and see the adjudication requirement for their condemnation, which is doom and destruction of their personal Spirit in the Second Death. And any good they did will not be remembered to save them from certain destruction for not accepting to live by HIS New Covenant to Honor HIS Son and that is the Testimony of our GOD the Father, which HE provided for us to have eternal Life. Those who ignore this Word of Truth will not see eternal Life in the Kingdom of GOD.

They will be executed to die the Second Death, the death of their evil personal Spirit. Their evil Spirit will be destroyed like useless cut-off Branches that did not bear fruit and are gathered together to be consumed by fire and cease to exist. They will not enter eternal Life in the New Kingdom of our GOD the Father because there is no place for the evil in them to exist in Heaven. And their Names will be blotted out in the Book of Life to be forgotten forever. They will no longer hurt, torment, and lead astray the Holy Children of our GOD the Father who are anointed with HIS Holy Spirit and the Spirit of our Lord Jesus Christ.

This is the Word, and it is the Truth.

Just as Peter was told by our Lord Jesus Christ: "Unless I wash you, you have no part with Me". Of course, Peter did not fully understand the lesson yet, but he has faith in our Lord Jesus Christ, and he has trust in Him, enough to have changed his heart and mind anyway. This is why we must remember to take the time that we need to stay connected to our Lord Jesus Christ every day like fruit-bearing Branches on the Vine, by praying in our Spirit with the Holy Spirit to learn the Word of Truth by heart. And by sharing the Word to learn it together, we help wash one another with the love of the Truth in the Word to keep us Holy in Christ Jesus, just as we are commanded to do by our Lord Jesus Christ.

And our Lord Jesus Christ speaks the Word into our hearts through the Holy Spirit living in us to continue to make our GOD the Father known to the World through us, and we may become stronger in faith to use the Word to protect our eternal Life that we have now, as we suffer to share the Word of Truth with the people of the World who are being called by our GOD the Father through our Lord Jesus Christ.

- ### Romans 10:17 (NIV)
    17 Consequently, faith comes from hearing the message, and the message is heard through the Word about Christ.

- ### John 6:37:40 (NIV)
    37 All those the Father gives Me will come to Me, and whoever comes to Me I will never drive away. (Jesus Christ). 38 For I have come down from Heaven not to do My will but to do the will of HIM who sent Me. 39 And this is the will of HIM (GOD the Father) who sent Me, that I shall lose none of all those HE has given Me, but raise them up at the Last Day. 40 For My Father's will is that everyone who looks to the Son and believes in Him shall have eternal Life, and I will raise them up at the Last Day."

This is the Word, and it is the Truth.

Our GOD the Father sent our Lord Jesus Christ, and gave us all to Him, and He will not lose any of us, He will raise us up at the Last Day to eternal Life without sin or fault. And on that Last Day the wicked and

Chapter 1: His Last Hours Begin

all evil ones that refuse to believe in our Lord Jesus Christ will also be raised up to Judgment for their condemnation to be destroyed. (executed)

As we read on, keep in mind, Satan the devil was already at work with (Judas-Iscariot) by prompting him with a plan to turn against the Apostles and have our Lord Jesus Christ arrested by giving away His location. Yet, our Lord Jesus Christ did not stop teaching the Apostles to fulfill His commands from our GOD the Father to help the Apostles believe in Him. And He loved them to the end of His Life in the flesh with them.

And This Is Our Prayer:

We pray in Spirit to give thanks to You, our GOD the Father, for having mercy on us by sending our Lord Jesus Christ from Your glorious presence in Heaven to save us in the World.

We thank You for giving us Your Word of Truth through Him, for our sanctification and salvation.

We accept Your Testimony to believe in our Lord Jesus Christ, that He was sent by You with the Life you put in Him for our salvation from sin and death to cross over to eternal Life now.

We ask You to keep us in Your love and bless us by Your Holy Spirit within us to guide us for eternal Life in complete unity with You.

We pray to ask You in the NAME of Your only begotten Son, our Lord Jesus Christ.

Chapter 2: The Betrayers Plan Foretold

John 13:18-30 NIV

18 I am not referring to all of you; I know those I have chosen. But this is to fulfill this passage of scripture: 'He who shared my bread has turned against me.'

19 "I am telling you now before it happens, so that when it does happen you will believe that I am who I am.

20 **Very truly I tell you**, whoever accepts anyone I send accepts Me; and whoever accepts Me accepts the One who sent Me."

21 After He had said this, Jesus was troubled in Spirit and Testified, "**Very truly I tell you**, one of you is going to betray Me."

22 His disciples stared at one another, at a loss to know which of them He meant. **23** One of them, the disciple whom Jesus loved, was reclining next to Him. **24** Simon Peter motioned to this disciple and said, "Ask Him which one He means."

25 Leaning back against Jesus, he asked Him, "Lord, who is it?"

26 Jesus answered, "It is the one to whom I will give this piece of bread when I have dipped it in the dish." Then, dipping the

Chapter 2: The Betrayers Plan Foretold

piece of bread, He gave it to Judas, the son of Simon Iscariot.

27 As soon as Judas took the bread, Satan entered into him. So, Jesus told him, "What you are about to do, do quickly."

28 But no one at the meal understood why Jesus said this to him.

29 Since Judas had charge of the money, some thought Jesus was telling him to buy what was needed for the festival, or to give something to the poor. **30** As soon as Judas had taken the bread, he went out. And it was night."

❖ Notice:

Our Lord Jesus Christ proves once again, that He was sent by our GOD the Father and that our GOD the Father was doing HIS works through our Lord Jesus Christ, by foretelling the future about what was written in prophecy would happen very soon, and later about the betrayal against Him would be carried out by one of the disciples.

Prophesy is given for many to tell, but the exact day, time, and details is only known by the eternal One, our GOD the Father. And our Lord Jesus Christ glorified our GOD the Father in Him, by giving this message to the disciples in advance, to help them believe that He was sent by our GOD the Father when the prophecy was fulfilled, and it gets revealed to them. It's the same way our lives are when we worship and pray in Spirit to our GOD the Father in the NAME of HIS Son Jesus Christ, and the things we need to be adjusted in our Life are corrected by the power of our GOD the Father and revealed to us after all the work HE has done to bless us is completed.

He establishes our steps and makes our paths straight for us to keep us Holy and safe in HIS care from the evil one. Keep in mind, even in His last day the disciples were all still trying to believe without a doubt, that our Lord Jesus Christ was sent from our GOD the Father in Heaven for our salvation and that He is the first and only begotten Son of our GOD the Father through whom all things were created.

That is why He told them in advance and in detail about events they would see happen to Him; and when they did come true, they would believe in Him. And the Holy Spirit will also testify about Him to you, as He lives in you, and you live in the Spirit. So, you also will believe without a doubt when it is revealed to you that everything our Lord Jesus Christ said would happen is happening.

This is the Word, and it is the Truth.

- ### Luke 18 N.I.V.
    31 Jesus took the twelve aside and told them, "We are going up to Jerusalem, and everything that is written by the prophets about the Son of Man will be fulfilled. 32 (Jesus Christ) He will be delivered over to the Gentiles. They will mock Him, insult Him and spit on Him; 33 They will flog Him and kill Him. On the third day He will rise again."

At that time, our Lord Jesus Christ was still teaching the Apostles to believe in Him and to believe the Testimony of our GOD the Father concerning Himself. Our Lord Jesus Christ felt troubled in Spirit, because He knew who the betrayer was, and that Satan was nearby to possess the betrayer Judas Iscariot' Then He revealed to the Apostles that it was (Judas-Iscariot) that would betray Him when He shared His food with Judas.

The so called, prince of this World, Satan, who is the devil, had already prompted Judas with a plan to give away their location; and then, at that time, Satan entered into Judas to carry out the betrayal plan against our

Chapter 2: The Betrayers Plan Foretold

Lord Jesus Christ. That night, they all witnessed the prophecy being fulfilled, exactly as what our Lord Jesus Christ foretold would happen.

Judas decided for himself to allow Satan's evil Spirit to possess him when he decided not to follow our Lord Jesus Christ and follow the evil ways of Satan. Judas accepted to stay condemned and be evil himself, and that leads to doom and destruction for anyone who does the same as Judas.

Your Life is who you believe in and follow, and Judas followed the way of the World that hates our Lord Jesus Christ. Anyone living without our Lord Jesus Christ in them, have no protection from evil in them and they are condemned already in the flesh. Remember, believers are protected from evil when we decide to accept the Holy Spirit within us; that is the Holy Spirit sent by our Lord Jesus Christ from out of our GOD the Father. Whoever the Holy Spirit rests within are then given the Right to be a Child of GOD the Father and no evil can enter there in them.

The Holy Spirit is the Seal of our GOD the Father, and every believer is marked with HIS Seal in our Lord Jesus Christ as a Holy Child belonging to our Almighty GOD the Father for eternal Life with a promise for redemption to enter HIS New Kingdom. You can believe in your heart and say, "I am a Child of GOD the Father and HIS Holy Spirit lives in me." And if you cannot speak, the Holy Spirit will testify for you from your heart that you are a Holy Spirit Child of GOD.

This is the Word, and it is the Truth.

- Romans 8:16-17 (NIV)
  16 The Spirit Himself Testifies with our Spirit that we are GOD'S Children. 17 Now if we are Children, then we are Heirs—Heirs of GOD and Co-Heirs with Christ, if indeed we share in His sufferings in order that we may also share in His glory.

- **James 1:21 (NIV)**
  21 Therefore, get rid of all moral filth and the evil that is so prevalent, and humbly accept the Word planted in you, which can save you.

We must keep the Word of GOD the Father every day to rid our soul of sin, weakness, and doubt. So, we may become stronger to our fullest potential in faith, that way we will live in Spirit to please our GOD the Father for eternal Life.

- **Mark 11:24 (NIV)**
  24 Therefore I tell you, whatever you ask for in prayer, believe that you have received it, and it will be yours. And when you stand praying, if you hold anything against anyone, forgive them, so that your Father in Heaven may forgive you your sin."

Forgive others so you can be forgiven because we are not judges and we are commanded by our Lord Jesus Christ to always love each other. Pray in Spirit for those that do wrong to you, forgive them for their sin, then you will be in good standing with a pure heart. And by asking in prayer without any doubt, in the NAME of our Lord Jesus Christ, you glorify our GOD the Father and HE will hear you, in Spirit prayer. Because you are HIS child, and you do not ever doubt HIM.

Do not believe the lies of how the World portrays our Lord Jesus Christ as weak and frail. Do not confuse His kindness with weakness. Our Lord

Chapter 2: The Betrayers Plan Foretold

Jesus Christ was fearless then, and is fearless today, now, and forever. He loves us so much, that He did what He had to do because He was willingly fulfilling many prophesies concerning Himself; including the prophecy to be tortured to death for us; so He may be resurrected by the Holy Spirit of our GOD the Father and be glorified with the power of Life in Him to forgive us for our sin. The sin that we committed and then sincerely repented.

There is no sin in us with our Lord Jesus Christ living in us. He accepted you as you were, with all your sin in you, when you called on His NAME from your heart in prayer to Him, our GOD the Father heard you and answered your call for help from HIM. Now that you have HIS attention, keep learning what is expected of you living by the Word of Truth and do it, so you don't get cut off from eternal Life. And you prayed in Spirit, by the way you learned the message in the Word, to believe in Him and our GOD the Father, who both are Spirit. And HE is looking for the kind of worshippers that worship HIM in Spirit.

True believers, who know our GOD the Father, learned the Word and how to always pray to worship our GOD the Father in Spirit through the NAME of our Lord Jesus Christ, HIS Son, to remain in complete unity with THEM. And He heard your prayer the first time you believed the Testimony of GOD the Father without a doubt, and He washed all your sin away to make you a Holy Child of GOD with the Right to enter HIS Kingdom.

Believe that you now stand Holy with our Lord Jesus Christ in complete unity in you, and you in Him.

- **1 John 5:10-12 (NIV)**

  10 Whoever believes in the Son of GOD accepts this, Testimony. Whoever does not believe GOD has made HIM out to be a liar, because they have not believed the

Testimony GOD has given about HIS Son. 11 And this is the Testimony: GOD has given us eternal Life, and this Life is in HIS Son. 12 Whoever has the Son has Life; whoever does not have the Son of GOD does not have Life.

———

Those who have the Spirit of our Lord Jesus Christ living in them know He is living in them because He is constantly working through us to glorify our GOD the Father in everything we say and do. We pray to our GOD the Father and ask for HIS guidance in Spirit, and HIS Holy Spirit within us tells us our Choice of words or deeds that we must do to please our GOD the Father. Now strengthen your faith by contemplating the Word every day, because you are being saved with the Holy Spirit of Our GOD the Father living in you and helping you. You are living Holy in complete unity with THEIR power, love, and self-control in you helping you live Holy every moment of your life.

Sin was in you before, and now it is gone because our Lord Jesus Christ forgave you for your sin and will live in you only without any sin in you. And He will allow you to live in Him only without any sin in you, so you may remain Holy and united with Him. That is why you must humble yourself and forgive everyone who has done anything against you before you pray in Spirit to our GOD the Father, in the NAME of HIS Son, our Lord Jesus Christ. So, HE will hear your prayers, you must worship the Holy in Spirit because that is the kind of worshippers our GOD the Father is looking for.

Therefore, HE gave us our Lord Jesus Christ, who washes your sin away with His authority of forgiveness to make you a Holy Child of GOD. And now He lives in you, as One with you, as you live in Him in complete unity with the Holy Spirit.

This is the Word, and it is the Truth.

You are saved from judgment and shame, which is doom and destruction

Chapter 2: The Betrayers Plan Foretold

when you appear Holy with our Lord Jesus Christ and the Holy Spirit in you at the Throne of Righteousness, the judgment Seat, the Bema Seat, the Throne of our Lord Jesus Christ to see Him in His glory in Heaven in the presence of our GOD the Father. Then you will rejoice, and praise Him because there is no sin or fault to be found in you to judge you by; for He has made you Holy on Earth first, and then He will redeem you with your reward in Heaven for living and remaining Holy in complete unity.

You will be given the Crown of Glory for your Decision to live in righteousness and in Spirit. That is the reward of redemption, not to be confused with judgment. As our Lord said, those that believe in Him, will not be judged; they will not see judgment or shame. The inspiration for eternal Life is in the glory of our Lord Jesus Christ living within every believer in Him. He is your Life, and you must have Him living in you to have His glory of eternal Life in you giving Life to you forever. He is Life in you, and you are Life with Him.

- ### Acts 4:11-12 (NIV)
  11 Jesus is "'the stone you builders rejected, which has become the Cornerstone.' 12 Salvation is found in no one else, for there is no other NAME under Heaven given to Mankind by which we must be saved."

Our Lord Jesus Christ suffered to death as a Sin Offering for us to have eternal Life. He was lethally whipped repeatedly with whips made with metal hooks and beads that stripped the skin and flesh from His body from head to foot, front and back, and on each side, before He was nailed to a crucifix to bleed out to His death from the injuries he sustained. Then He committed His Spirit to our GOD the Father at the moment He died without sin.

At His death, many supernatural things were happening that proved He is the Son of GOD. Many people must come to terms with how His death marks the beginning of the way we worship our GOD the FATHER through our Lord Jesus Christ, and the end of the old way we conducted ceremonies. That is why the curtain in the Temple was torn in two from top to bottom, not by people, but by the angels of GOD. Those old ways are over and the World can go to GOD through our Lord Jesus Christ at any time they want to. This is the New Covenant we have been given by our GOD the Father to live by at this appointed time.

He willingly sacrificed Himself without sin in Him. And by being the Sin Offering sent from our GOD the Father, our GOD the Father condemned sin in the flesh with the Blood Sacrifice of our Lord Jesus Christ to cleans us of all our sin and for us to be made Holy Children of GOD with HIS Holy Spirit dwelling in us. But only those who believe the Testimony of our GOD the Father and believe in HIM with enough faith to follow HIS commands. This is the will of our GOD the Father and our Lord Jesus Christ, that we have eternal Life. And anyone who accepts and believes the Testimony of our GOD, the Father, is made Holy by HIM through our Lord Jesus Christ. Believe in THEM, repent your sins in Spirit prayer, giving thanks to our GOD the Father in the NAME of HIS Son Jesus Christ, and by the authority given to our Lord Jesus Christ, your sins will be forgiven to live the Holy Life that you are called to have now.

Your eternal Life and the Life of your children, and everyone that you can help in your future is depending on you to turn to our Lord Jesus Christ, first for eternal Life in you, and then to help them turn to Him to have eternal Life in themselves.

- ### Mathew 27:50-53 (NIV)
  50 And when Jesus had cried out again in a loud voice, when He gave up His Spirit. 51 At that moment, the Curtain of the Temple was torn in two from top to bottom. The Earth shook,

Chapter 2: The Betrayers Plan Foretold

> *the rocks split, 52 and the tombs broke open. The bodies of many Holy People who had died were raised to Life. 53 They came out of the tombs after Jesus' resurrection and went into the Holy City and appeared to many people.*

Our Lord Jesus Christ never sinned. For that He was given all authority over all Heaven, and Earth, and Under Earth to reconcile all things to our GOD the Father.

Always be fearless as our Lord Jesus Christ is fearless living in you. And be filled with the spiritual power from the baptism of having the Holy Spirit of our GOD the Father that is living in you as well, as your personal Spirit lives as One with THEM. Now THEY live with your Spirit as One, just as our Lord Jesus Christ prayed to our GOD the Father for us to be One with THEM as THEY are One. We are now saved, and being saved from evil, sin, and death, for our redemption as Holy Children of GOD the Father. Keep HIS commands and, "Always Love Each Other."

And This Is Our Prayer:

We ask You, praying in Spirit, our GOD the Father, in the NAME of our Lord Jesus Christ, to send Your Holy Spirit into everyone that we love so they may be filled with the power of Your Holy Spirit to help reconcile others with you.

We accept Your Word of Truth that was brought to us by our Lord Jesus Christ. We grow stronger in faith each day as we keep Your Word with Your New Command to always love each other as the way we show our love to You and Your Son, our Lord Jesus Christ. We pray in Spirit to ask You in the NAME of Your Son, our Lord Jesus Christ.

Chapter 3: The NEW Commandment

John 13:31-38 NIV

31 When he, was gone, Jesus said, "Now the Son of Man (Jesus Christ) is glorified, and GOD is glorified in Him.

32 If GOD is glorified in Him, GOD will glorify the Son in HIMSELF and will glorify Him at once.

33 "My Children, I will be with you only a little longer. You will look for Me, and just as I told the Jews, so I tell you now: Where I am going, you cannot come.

34 A **New Command** I give you: **Love One Another**. As I have loved you, So, you must Love One Another.

35 By this everyone will know that you are My disciples, if you Love One Another."

36 Simon Peter asked Him, "Lord, where are you going?" Jesus replied, "Where I am going, you cannot follow now, but you will follow later."

37 Peter asked, "Lord, why can't I follow you now? I will lay down my life for You."

38 Then Jesus answered, "Will you really lay down your life for Me? **Very truly I tell you**, Before the rooster crows, you will disown Me three times!

Chapter 3: The New Commandment

❖ **Notice:**

After our Lord Jesus Christ saw Satan enter into Judas Iscariot to execute the betrayal plan, He waited for the evil ones to leave, before He would address the disciples again.

First, He glorified our GOD the Father in Him by foretelling and then fulfilling the prophecy, which proved He was sent by our GOD the Father, and that He knew everything by our GOD the Father working through Him, including what is to become of everything in the future. Because our GOD the Father is living in Him with HIS Holy Spirit to do HIS work for our salvation, and the same Holy Spirit that is in Him, is also in us, and our Lord Jesus Christ tells us through the Holy Spirit what we need to know in advance to help us keep our faith while living by the Word in the Spirit.

We must think of the words, "alive in, or living in," each other when our Lord Jesus Christ teaches us about being in complete unity with THEM when He teaches us about being One with each other by a miraculous Spirit connection that only our GOD the Father allows by HIS Holy Spirit that HE chooses to put in us to dwell in us and work directly with our personal Spirit in our Body-Temple. Our Lord Jesus Christ explains it like this, "The Father is in Me, and I am in Him. And I am in you, and you are in Me."

Complete unity means we are "alive and living" in each other by the Holy Spirit, with our Lord Jesus Christ and His Spirit with His Life in us, and our GOD the Father in Him; and the Holy Spirit of our GOD the Father is living within each of us all, which makes us living in complete unity with THEM living in us for eternal Life. By the power of Life in them living in us is how our personal Spirits are blessed and protected by the NAME of our Lord Jesus Christ now at this appointed time living on Earth and beyond after we are resurrected by the Voice of our Lord Jesus Christ calling us up to meet Him in the cloud for our redemption to appear Holy with Him in the presence our GOD the Father. THEY are alive and living in us, with THEIR powerful Spirits, without any sin in us. We are blessed and Holy as we live in the Spirit with THEM in our Body-Temple at this appointed time where we will be blessed throughout our lifetime now.

We have crossed over from death to Life and we will not be judged or put to any shame when we see our Lord Jesus Christ in His glory in Heaven on His Throne because we have repented and have been legitimately forgiven for our sin by the authority given to our Lord Jesus Christ from our merciful GOD the Father who loves us and wants us to live with HIM now. We will appear Holy without sin, accusation, or fault, to receive from Him the Crown of Life and glorify Him and our GOD the Father forever.

Praise be to our GOD the Father in the NAME of His Son, our Lord Jesus Christ forever. We are saved because we have our Lord Jesus Christ alive in us by the will of our GOD the Father who created us all to have eternal Life. And those that refuse to believe in Him and decided not to have our Lord Jesus Christ in themselves, are condemned already and awaiting judgment for the execution of their personal Spirit to their Second Death. There is no eternal Life in them because our Lord Jesus Christ who carries the power of Life in Himself does not dwell in the bodies of non-believers.

- **1 Corinthians 6:18-20 (NIV)**
  18 Flee from sexual immorality. All other sins a person commits are outside the body, but whoever sins sexually, sins against their own body. 19 Do you not know that your bodies are Temples of the Holy Spirit, who is in you, whom you have received from GOD? You are not your own; 20 You were bought at a price. Therefore, honor GOD with your bodies.

Chapter 3: The New Commandment

- **John 8:42-47 (N.I.V.**

    42 Jesus said to them, "If GOD were your Father, you would love Me, for I have come from GOD. I have not come on My own; 'GOD sent Me.' 43 Why is My language not clear to you? Because you are unable to Hear what I say. 44 You belong to your father, the devil (Satan), and you want to carry out your father's (Satan) desires. He was a murderer from the beginning, not holding to the Truth, for there is no Truth in him. When he lies, he speaks his native language, for he is a liar and the father of Lies. 45 Yet because I tell the Truth, you do not believe Me! 46 Can any of you prove Me guilty of sin? If I am telling the Truth, why don't you believe Me? 47 Whoever belongs to GOD hears what GOD says. The reason you do not hear is that you do not belong to GOD."

Just as the Testimony of our GOD the Father is written in the Word: No one can have eternal Life if they do not have our Lord Jesus Christ living in themself; with the Holy Spirit of our GOD the Father dwelling in their Body-Temple now, already forgiven for sin, without fault, or accusation, and living Holy in complete unity with THEM. And because we are Servants of our GOD the Father and follow His Son, our Lord Jesus Christ, we are living a spiritual Life with our Lord Jesus Christ in us and our GOD the Father in Him and His Holy Spirit in complete unity. We are saved now on Earth to be redeemed later in Heaven, forever.

- **Galatians 6:7-8 (NIV)**

    7 Do not be deceived: GOD cannot be mocked. A man reaps what he sows. 8 Whoever sows to please their flesh, from the flesh will reap destruction; whoever sows to please the Spirit, from the Spirit will reap eternal life.

Keep in mind, that the Holy Spirit is also in us, guiding us, interceding our thoughts, prayers, and needs from our heart to our GOD the Father, while teaching us the Word, and telling us what our Lord Jesus Christ wants us to know. And by planting in our hearts what we learn from the Word by the guidance of the Holy Spirit we will reap eternal Life now on Earth. And after we are called up and raised up by the Voice of our Lord Jesus Christ to see Him at His glorious Throne in Heaven, He will reward us with the Crown of eternal Life. Then we will enter the New Kingdom to live with our GOD the Father in peace.

We must justify what is in our heart, by our own belief to live in Spirit, by acting on our own Decision to submit and commit our Spirit to our GOD the Father, and ask of HIM on our own behalf to be guided by His Holy Spirit; His Holy Spirit who now gives us our Choices in our lives, of what we must say in words and the deeds that we must do in good faith. Our GOD the Father gave us the Choice as a gift; we believe in Him, and it was our Decision to be guided by His Holy Spirit while living in the Spirit. Because we know Him and we are not our own, we belong to our GOD the Father as HIS Servant. We will not do our own schemes and plans by our own choices, No! not anymore. Because we are not our own, we belong to our GOD the Father and we only say and do HIS will. To the glory of our GOD the Father!

This is His Word, and it is His Truth.

We must listen for what HIS Holy Spirit is telling us our Choices are, because it is everything that our Lord Jesus Christ tells Him to tell us, in what to say and do to glorify our GOD the Father.

We must only do and say what our Lord Jesus Christ tells us to do and say, giving thanks and praise and glory to our GOD the Father in spiritual prayer, in the NAME of our Lord Jesus Christ, as we live in the Spirit with THEM. That is the kind of worshiper our GOD the Father is looking for.

Chapter 3: The New Commandment

This is the Word, and it is the Truth.

Then our Lord Jesus Christ gave us a New Command for us to keep: **"Love One Another"**. He tells us how much to love each other in the very next verse: "As I have loved you, so you must Love One Another." And then He explains what others will think of our family when we always love each other. "By this everyone will know you are My disciples." We are His disciples as we learn and help teach the message in His Word for others to know our GOD the Father and our Lord Jesus Christ for eternal Life in themselves.

The Old Covenant in all its glory brought death. Our GOD the Father did make a change. He made and gave us the "New Covenant," through His Son, our Lord Jesus Christ. As it is written in the New Testament. And it is appropriate to now have a New Command. And that is to "Love One Another" as our Lord Jesus Christ says to do. If we did not need a New Command, our Lord Jesus Christ would not have said it. As it is, it is so important in the Word that our Lord Jesus Christ said, "I give you a New Command!" And that is: **"Love One Another."** And that is the deed we are expected to do with the inspiration of our faith from the wisdom of knowing the message in the Word.

Keep His commands to show you love Him and always love each other. Saying that you have faith and are saved, without doing deeds, is not faith; it is worthless. Being that way is only keeping the Word a secret from the World the way Satan does. Satan and demons know the Word is the Truth and they want us not to speak the Word of Truth. They know that there is only One GOD, who sent His Son and NAMED Him Jesus Christ. They have seen THEM both in Heaven, before Satan and the demons lost their place in heaven, when they were Angels and cast out of Heaven to Earth. But they keep the Truth to themselves, like a secret from Mankind, to lead as many as they can astray from turning to our Lord Jesus Christ.

INSPIRATION FOR YOUR ETERNAL LIFE

Anyone who refuses to keep the commands is condemned already, where they stand condemned by their own decision. And their evil deeds are to keep speaking lies to you, to have you remain ignorant of the Truth and keep you in sin to lead your Spirit astray to your death. And that is standing condemned now awaiting to be Executed later, on the Judgement Day, at the Judgement Seat of our Lord Jesus Christ. All Mankind are already condemned without believing what the Testimony of our GOD the Father says, and by not doing what it takes to have our Lord Jesus Christ, and that is having His Son living in our Body-Temple now. It is only required for us to believe in Him and Decide to go to our Lord Jesus Christ for Life.

Our GOD the Father made this choice for us. His Choice for us is to have Life through His Son, our Lord Jesus Christ living in us with the Holy Spirit of our GOD the Father in complete unity. When an evil one tries to approach you with their lies, reproach them with the Word of Truth, and they will flee from you, because they have no power over you, as you are living in our Lord Jesus Christ in unity.

We do not fear Satan; our Lord Jesus Christ commands us and says, "Do not fear." We have our Lord Jesus Christ living in us as we speak about the Word against any lies. That is how the Word will save your life. We have the power of GOD in the NAME of our Lord Jesus Christ protecting us to resist the evil one. Our faith is strengthened by constantly learning and believing the Word in your hearts, and proclaiming it with your Mouth, first to be saved ourselves. If you cannot speak, then write it or text it. The point is to help Others know the Gospel of our Lord Jesus Christ and believe in Him by what He teaches us to receive the Holy Spirit of our GOD the Father. By doing what the Word instructs us to do is the true Faith that can save the lives of others, and by that, our own life is kept saved for doing what we can do to Help Others believe.

- **Mathew 10:32-33 (NIV)**
    32 "*Whoever acknowledges Me before others, I will also*

Chapter 3: The New Commandment

acknowledge before My Father in Heaven. 33 But whoever disowns Me before others, I will disown before My Father in Heaven.

Those that are ashamed to speak the Gospel are disowning our Lord Jesus Christ before others. By Teaching others, the Gospel that you learned is acknowledging our Lord Jesus Christ before others. Those acts of proclaiming the Truth from you are what pleases our GOD the Father, and He rewards those who do His deeds with eternal Life.

This is the Word, and it is the Truth.

- Matthew 22:36-40 (NIV)
    36 "Teacher, which is the greatest commandment in the Law?" 37 Jesus replied: **"Love the LORD your GOD with all your heart and with all your Soul and with all your Mind."** *38 This is the first and greatest commandment. 39 And the second is like it:* **"Love your neighbor as yourself"** *40 All the Law and the prophets hang on these two commandments."*

As disciples of our Lord Jesus Christ, we keep these two commands that are written in the Word. All Believers believe in the Testimony of our GOD the Father concerning HIS Son, our Lord Jesus Christ. And we know them by heart so we may help others understand the Word is the Truth. Because we must know the Word to understand the Truth in it, before we can do what it says to do, and live by it in the Spirit.

- James 4:15-17 (NIV)
    15 Instead, you ought to say, "If it is the Lord's will, we will live and do this or that." 16 As it is, you boast in your arrogant schemes. All such boasting is evil. 17 If anyone, then, knows the good they ought to do

and doesn't do it, it is sin for them.

- ## James 1:12 (NIV)
  <u>12</u> Blessed is the one who perseveres under trial because, having stood the test, that person will receive the Crown of Life that the Lord has promised to those who love Him.

- ## James 1:21 (NIV)
  21...humbly accept the Word planted in you, which can save you.

(The Testimony of our GOD the Father)

- ## 1 John 5:11-12 (NIV)
  <u>11</u> And this is the Testimony: GOD has given us eternal Life, and this Life is in HIS Son. <u>12</u> Whoever has the Son has Life; whoever does not have the Son of GOD, does not have Life.

Accept our Lord Jesus Christ with the Word He brought to us from our GOD the Father in Heaven, for eternal Life. He was sent by our GOD the Father to teach us the Testimony of our GOD the Father. Because it is the will of our GOD the Father for us to receive eternal Life. Doing what the Word says can save your life and keep you from straying away from the path that leads us to eternal Life living with our GOD the Father. It is written within the Word; we must keep His commands if we love our Lord Jesus Christ. It is not good enough just to know the Word, you must live by it and do what it says to do.

- ## James 1:22-25 (NIV)

Chapter 3: The New Commandment

22 Do not merely listen to the Word, and so deceive yourselves, do what it says. 23 Anyone who listens to the Word but does not do what it says is like someone who looks at his face in a mirror 24 and, after looking at himself, goes away and immediately forgets what he looks like. 25 But whoever looks intently into the perfect Law (New Covenant) that gives freedom, and continues in it—not forgetting what they have heard, but doing it— they will be blessed in what they do.

- ### James 2:18-19 (NIV)

  18 But someone will say, "you have faith; I have deeds." Show me your faith without deeds, and I will show you my faith by my deeds. 19 You believe that there is One GOD. Good! Even the demons believe that—and shudder.

- ### James 2:26 (NIV)

  26 As the body without the Spirit is dead, So, faith without deeds is dead.

- ### John 14:15-17 (NIV)

  15 "If you love Me, keep My commands. 16 And I will ask the Father, and He will give you Another Advocate to help you and be with you forever— 17 The Spirit of Truth. (Holy Spirit) The World cannot accept Him because it neither sees Him nor knows Him. But you know Him, for He lives with you and will be in you.

Remember the New Command given by our Lord Jesus Christ and **Always Love Each Other**.

And This Is Our Prayer:

We pray in Spirit to ask You, our GOD the Father, to sanctify our Body-Temple with Your Word of Truth, as we learn Your Word by heart and live by the New Command to Always Love Each Other. May Your Spirit of Truth guide our Spirit within us, while we help others learn to know Your Son, our Lord Jesus Christ and You, our GOD the Father, by Your Testimony and Your Word of Truth.

We believe that You sent Your Son Jesus Christ from Heaven with Your Word to save us through Him. And with the authority You gave Him, He may give eternal life to whomever believes in Him, because You gave Him the power of Life that is from You, and You put it in Him. By having Your Son, our Lord Jesus Christ in us, is having eternal Life in us.

We pray to ask You in the NAME of Your Son, our Lord Jesus Christ.

Chapter 4: Believe and Follow Jesus Christ to GOD the Father

John 14:1-14 NIV

1 "Do not let your hearts be troubled. You believe in GOD. believe also in Me.

2 My Father's house has many rooms; if that were not so, would I have told you that I am going there to prepare a place for you?

3 And if I go and prepare a place for you, I will come back and take you to be with Me that you also may be where I am.

4 You know the Way to the place where I am going."

5 Thomas said to Him, "Lord, we don't know where You are going, so how can we know the Way?"

6 Jesus answered, "I am the Way and the Truth and the Life. No one comes to the Father except through Me.

7 If you really know Me, you will know My Father as well. From now on, you do know HIM and have seen HIM."

8 Philip said, "Lord, show us the Father and that will be enough for us."

9 Jesus answered: "Don't you know Me, Philip, even after I have been among you such a long time? Anyone who has seen Me has

Chapter 4: Believe and Follow Jesus Christ...

seen the Father. How can you say, 'Show us the Father'?

<u>10</u> Don't you believe that I am in the Father, and that the Father is in Me? The Words I say to you I do not speak on My own authority. Rather, it is the Father, living in Me, who is doing HIS work.

<u>11</u> Believe Me when I say that I am in the Father and the Father is in Me; or at least believe on the evidence of the works themselves.

<u>12</u> **Very truly I tell you**, whoever believes in Me will do the works I have been doing, and they will do even greater things than these, because I am going to the Father.

<u>13</u> And I (Jesus Christ) will do whatever you ask in My NAME, so that the Father may be glorified in the Son.

<u>14</u> You may ask Me for anything in My NAME, and I will do it.

❖ Notice:

Our Lord Jesus Christ tells us, "Do not let your hearts be troubled." He does not want us to be afraid, worried, weak, or fall away from the Word of Truth to lose faith. So, He tells us how everything will work out for us, and how to keep our faith strong in the Word of Truth; by believing the message in the Word and doing what it says to do. That is the New Covenant of our GOD the Father, that we have and believe in our Lord Jesus Christ and do what He teaches us in the Word.

We must learn the Gospel and the Word by heart, to remain believing in our Savior, Teacher, and Lord Jesus Christ. And believe that our GOD the Father has sent Him to us from Heaven, which was the hardest thing for the Apostles to believe. They believed in our GOD the Father, but they did not believe anyone could be that close to our GOD the Father, to be HIS only begotten Son, and then sent from Heaven. Their faith was only in believing in our GOD the Father based on the Old Covenant. So, it was difficult for them to change what they already believed in their Heart, Soul, and Mind.

They never heard of the Testimony of our GOD the Father or the New Covenant. They didn't have a New Testament because they were the Chosen Ones to be a witness to our Lord Jesus Christ and send their letters out into the World as their Testimony to teach us by the power of our GOD the Father and HIS Holy Spirit sent by our Lord Jesus Christ. Their Testimony is the Gospel of our Lord Jesus Christ written for the World to learn from. Their letters were carefully written while living in the Spirit with the guidance of the Holy Spirit and the Spirit of our Lord Jesus Christ within them, which were then collected and bound into books that we now have as the New Testament for us to be sanctified by, in learning the Word of our GOD the Father, to ready us to receive the salvation of baptism with the Holy Spirit by our Lord Jesus Christ, to live in complete unity with THEM in our Body-Temple now and forever.

The New Covenant and the Testimony of our GOD the Father concerning HIS Son, our Lord Jesus Christ, was all recent news to them being taught by our Teacher, Savior, and Lord Jesus Christ. And now that we have received the Holy Spirit, the Holy Spirit will help us learn the Word by writing it into our hearts, as He reminds us of everything our Lord Jesus Christ has taught us in the New Covenant. It was very difficult for them to change their minds and believe it in their heart until our Lord Jesus Christ revealed to them events in their future so accurately that they would have to believe in Him to be the Son of our GOD the Father, and that He was sent by our GOD the Father from Heaven to fulfill the New Covenant for our salvation to reconcile us with our GOD the Father in Heaven.

Chapter 4: Believe and Follow Jesus Christ...

We must all believe the Testimony of our GOD the Father and learn what HIS will is for sending our Lord Jesus Christ to us. HIS will is to give us eternal Life and HE has given it as a gift through HIS Son, Jesus Christ. In these scriptures, we learn how our salvation is accomplished and complete by understanding what we must do to remain Holy in our Lord Jesus Christ. This also means to at least know the message of the Word in your heart to recognize the Truth. Even if you cannot recite it verbatim, at least you know the Word is the Truth and believe in HIM. By accepting and believing in the Testimony of our GOD the Father concerning our Lord Jesus Christ is accepting and believing in the New Covenant. The New Covenant is of the Spirit that gives us life because we are living in Spirit with our Lord Jesus Christ in complete unity by keeping His commands.

The New Covenant is everything our GOD the Father has given to us through our Lord Jesus Christ to give us eternal Life. That is HIS will, and it has been HIS will before the World began. Only through our Lord Jesus Christ can we receive eternal Life to live Holy on Earth now, and after we are redeemed and transformed into imperishable Spirit-Bodies to live with THEM in the New Kingdom, on the New World that our GOD the Father will make for our home with HIM, for us to be with HIM forever. To have our Lord Jesus Christ living in us, is to have the New Covenant in our heart, which is to have eternal Life in complete unity with THEM.

Our Lord Jesus Christ has fulfilled the New Covenant with the righteousness within Himself by which He has overcome the World to reconcile all things to glorify our GOD the Father. Therefore, only through Him are we rightfully reconciled with our GOD the Father as HIS Holy Children. It is better to believe just enough of the Word in your heart and live by it for salvation than to know all the Bible verses, and not live in the New Covenant, to then stand condemned and awaiting execution by Judgement and shame on the Last Day. (Judgment Day) There is no salvation in knowing all the written laws. There is only salvation by believing in our Lord Jesus Christ and obeying His commands to remain united with Him. Our GOD the Father is always teaching us the meaning of Life. Believing in Him is to know everything by learning from HIM through our Lord Jesus Christ and the Seal of our GOD the Father.

The meaning of Life is to have eternal Life. To have eternal Life is to know our GOD the Father and HIS Son, our Lord Jesus Christ. To know our GOD the Father to is believe in HIS Testimony concerning HIS Son, our Lord Jesus Christ. To know our Lord Jesus Christ is to have the love and Spirit of our Lord Jesus Christ living in unity within you. To have our Lord Jesus Christ living within you is to live Holy by your Spirit living with the guidance of the Holy Spirit from our GOD the Father in complete unity within you now. To live in complete unity with THEM now is to have eternal Life.

We must live and pray spiritually in our Spirit that we were created with and accept to be united with our Lord Jesus Christ in us and to be guided by the Holy Spirit of our GOD the Father, who is also sent from out of our GOD the Father as our helper to be living within us. So, our Lord Jesus Christ will raise us up, first from amongst the dead in Christ, then the living in Jesus Christ for redemption to eternal Life by the Holy Spirit, just like He was raised up by the Holy Spirit of our GOD the Father at His appointed time from the cross.

It is only possible to be raised up to eternal Life in the New Kingdom after your Spirit is taken out of your flesh for your Mortal-Body to die and your Spirit is transformed into an imperishable Spirit-Body. Your eternal Life is justified by believing in our Lord Jesus Christ and by living in Spirit, united with our Lord Jesus Christ, who has the power of eternal Life in Him living within you now. This is called having our Lord Jesus Christ. And that is having Him in your life, living in your Body- Temple as One in complete unity, to include the Holy Spirit of our GOD the Father living in you, and helping you, and guiding your Spirit to remain Holy in the Church which is the Body of our Lord Jesus Christ. This is the Choice for eternal Life that our GOD the Father has

Chapter 4: Believe and Follow Jesus Christ...

given to us through our Lord Jesus Christ that we may receive by our Decision to live our lives believing in THEM. It is HIS choice for us and our Decision to accept HIS "New Covenant" as a gift.

There is no other Way to salvation without a relationship living with the Holy Spirit and living with our Lord Jesus Christ in you. All to the glory of our GOD the Father in heaven reconciling with us to bring Humanity back to HIMSELF. As our Lord Jesus Christ teaches us in the Word, anyone that does not have our Lord Jesus Christ living in unity with Him "stands condemned" already. If they stay ignorant by their Decision not to know and live in the Truth, then they will stay condemned for their life to end in destruction by their own selfish desires to remain unholy. When all they need to do is Decide to believe by the Testimony of our GOD the Father and Decide to accept HIS gift of eternal Life starting now. There is no other Way to our GOD the Father except through living in the Spirit of our Lord Jesus Christ in complete unity with our own personal Spirit that will remain alive in Him.

It's foolish to believe, that you can live by your own doctrine of a "self-righteous lifestyle", without actively serving our GOD the Father through having our Lord Jesus Christ in you; and then hope that your judgment of yourself by your own imagination is divine enough to regard yourself as righteous enough to be Crowned with eternal Life by our Lord Jesus Christ to stand Holy in the presence of our GOD the Father in heaven. That is not living by the commands or showing that you love our Lord Jesus Christ to others or sharing His love with others. No one, ever created by our God the Father has any power without our GOD the Father enabling them to by HIS Holy Spirit.

There is only one Way to eternal Life and that is what our GOD the Father Testified concerning our Lord Jesus Christ. A true believer knows it is the Word of Truth, and only with our Lord Jesus Christ in you now can you ever have eternal Life now and after Judgement Day. Living by "karma" is not salvation. That way of believing is a trap that leads to certain death. Because you are denying the help of our Lord Jesus Christ in yourself and "before others" by not Testifying to them about Him. You are doing nothing that way and doing nothing in faith without doing deeds to please the Spirit, which is not faith, and it leads to death. Faith without deeds is dead. And by living that cowardly way will result in you losing eternal Life for yourself and for everyone you love, that "could have" learned the Truth through your efforts to help them and their babies to have eternal Life in themselves.

The Truth is very simple to learn when you have our Lord Jesus Christ, so, you now know the Way to salvation, and then you must help others do the same, or it is sin for you not to do what you can do to help them. That is written in the Word, and our Lord Jesus Christ commands us to help others as He has helped us. Our Lord Jesus Christ warns us, that if anyone disowns Him, then He will disown them to our GOD the Father in Heaven. Without the help of our Lord Jesus Christ living in you now, you will have no part in Him, "now or later," for not believing in Him. Because we can do nothing without the power of our Lord Jesus Christ living with us.

Satan and his followers also know the message in the Word is the Truth. They call Him "Son of GOD" and fear Him, because they know they have an appointed time reserved for themselves to be executed on the Last Day for the sin and evil they committed. And they have put themselves above the Word of our GOD the Father, when they "Decided" not to obey HIS commands and live however they want. Now they stand condemned for their sin by not obeying and believing in the Testimony of our GOD the Father. To believe in the Word, we must 'live by it' and believe exactly like our Lord Jesus Christ does and teaches us to be, with one mind, in one faith, all in complete unity with us and the Holy Spirit of our GOD the Father in us. Serve all others above ourselves, to the glory of our GOD the Father, who is above all others first because HE is the creator of all things through HIS only begotten Son, our Lord Jesus Christ.

Chapter 4: Believe and Follow Jesus Christ...

- **Philippians 2:3-11 (NIV)**
  3 Do nothing out of selfish ambition or vain conceit. Rather, in humility value others above yourselves, 4 not looking to your own interests but each of you to the interests of the others. 5 In your relationships with one another, have the same mindset as Christ Jesus: 6 who, being in very nature GOD, did not consider equality with GOD something to be used to His own advantage; 7 rather, He made Himself nothing by taking the very nature of a servant, being made in Human likeness. 8 And being found in appearance as a Man, (Son of Man) He humbled Himself by becoming obedient to death— even death on a cross! 9 Therefore, GOD exalted Him to the Highest Place and gave Him the NAME that is above every name, 10 that at the NAME of Jesus every knee should bow, in Heaven and on Earth and Under the Earth, 11 and every tongue acknowledge that Jesus Christ is Lord, to the glory of GOD the Father.

- **Romans 8:16-17 (NIV)**
  16 The Spirit Himself testifies with our Spirit that we are GOD'S Children. 17 Now if we are Children, then we are Heirs— Heirs of GOD and Co-Heirs with Christ, if indeed we share in His sufferings in order that we may also share in His glory.

Believing is: Doing what our Lord Jesus Christ commands us to do in the Word He taught us out of our love for Him in our heart. When we do what we learned in the Word, we are following our Lord Jesus Christ straight to our GOD the Father for eternal Life. Our Lord Jesus Christ said, "I am the Way, the Truth, and the Life. No one comes to the Father except through Me."

"I am the Way-": because, only by having Him in us, and following through our Lord Jesus Christ, can we live a righteous life good enough to stand in the presence of our GOD the Father. Living by His Word is the Way, He taught us to live, and that shows that we love Him. By accepting Him we accept our GOD the Father. And when it is our appointed time, He will raise us up Holy, without sin or fault, or any shame from judgement. And we will appear together with the mark of HIS Seal on our foreheads and our Lord Jesus Christ in the presence of our GOD the Father.

"-and the Truth": because our GOD the Father sent our Lord Jesus Christ to be the Inspiration for our eternal Life by our having Him living in us and teaching us the Word of Truth to know how-to live according to the New Covenant. The Word is the Truth that we must learn to accept as truth in our hearts to believe in our Lord Jesus Christ and that He was sent by our GOD the Father.

"-and the Life.": because our GOD the Father gave HIS Son Jesus Christ the authority to Judge over Heaven and Earth and Under Earth. By that authority, our Lord Jesus Christ has been given eternal Life in Him, that He may give eternal Life to whomever believes in Him. He has the authority to Judge all the condemned who are to be executed to destruction on the Judgement Day for not believing in Him and living with their sin. Understand that, on the Last Day, eternal Life is for the Holy living in Christ Jesus; and eternal death is for the Spirits that reject to live in our Lord Jesus Christ. Our perfect Lord Jesus Christ is always waiting for us to turn to Him every day to embrace us with His love that gives us Life.

Therefore, He said, "No one comes to the Father except through Me.": because when our Lord Jesus Christ forgives us, He takes all our sin out of us for the Holy Spirit of our GOD the Father to come to us and rest within us. It is truly a miracle and a blessing that is given to us from our GOD the Father in Heaven through HIS Son, our Lord Jesus Christ for

Chapter 4: Believe and Follow Jesus Christ...

them to be living in us, in complete unity. We are then sanctified and forgiven for our salvation to be found without sin, or fault and have passed over from death to eternal Life already. That is how we are made Holy, living by our Spirit in our Body-Temple as One with THEM in us. That is living in complete unity with THEM, as our GOD the Father is living in us as One and dwelling in HIS Son, our Lord Jesus Christ.

Judgment and shame on the Judgement Day will pass over us because there is no sin or evil to be found in us anymore since our Lord Jesus Christ, who is living in us, has legitimately forgiven us for the sins we committed and repented by the authority bestowed in Him by our GOD the Father. Now the almighty power of eternal Life is living in Him and is also living in us giving us eternal Life in complete unity. The entire World of Humanity has fallen to death in disgrace by the lies of Satan. Only by believing and living by the Word in the New Covenant can we have salvation through the power in our Lord Jesus Christ. And only those that turn to our Lord Jesus Christ, first will understand His power to release us from the doom and destruction of our Spirit in the Second Death for sin, and then understand that by His will to do the will of our GOD the Father, He will restore everyone that lives by His commands to His perfection for eternal Life without judgment or shame.

This is the Word of our GOD the Father through our Lord Jesus Christ, and it is the Truth.

We are forgiven in our Lord Jesus Christ, just like one of the two men who were crucified next to our Lord Jesus Christ. Nothing is impossible with our Lord Jesus Christ living within us, in complete unity. He was forgiven for his sins and went straight to paradise that day and will be passed over for judgment on Judgement Day.

That day is also reserved for non-believers to be raised up, even from their graves to the Judgement Seat at their appointed time, the same as Satan and his evil spirit followers are all expecting to be consigned to the final place for execution to their destruction of their Spirit for their decision to stand condemned throughout their lifetime. That is judgment and shame for "their own decision" to keep living in their own sin.

- ## Luke 23:40-43 N.I.V.
    40 But the other criminal rebuked him. "Don't you fear GOD," he said, "since you are under the same sentence? 41 We are punished justly, for we are getting what our deeds deserve. But this Man has done nothing wrong." 42 Then he said, "Jesus, remember me when You come into Your Kingdom." 43 Jesus answered him, "Truly I tell you, Today you will be with Me in paradise."

Then when it is our appointed time, our Lord Jesus Christ will present us Holy to our GOD the Father without judgement and without shame.

- ## John 5:24-27 (NIV)
    *24 **"Very truly I tell you**, Whoever hears My Word and believes HIM who sent Me has eternal Life and will not be judged but has crossed over from death to Life. 25 **Very truly I tell you**, a time is coming and has now come when the dead will hear the Voice of the Son of GOD and those who hear will live. 26 For as the Father has Life in Himself, so, HE has granted the Son also to have Life in Himself. 27 And HE has given Him authority to judge because He is the Son of Man. ~ (Jesus Christ)*

Anyone who teaches otherwise is a false prophet who is confused by Satan into leading many people away from believing the Truth that is

Chapter 4: Believe and Follow Jesus Christ...

written in the Word of Salvation from our Lord Jesus Christ. Our Lord Jesus Christ teaches us, that the Words He spoke were not on His own authority. He tells us that He cannot do anything Himself except what our GOD the Father shows Him what He can and can't do. And now that He has returned and sits at the Right Side of our GOD the Father, He has been given that authority to do the will of our GOD the Father.

It is by the authority of our GOD the Father living in HIS Son Jesus Christ doing HIS work through HIS Son, our Lord Jesus Christ, as our GOD the Father is dwelling with HIS fullness of power "in" our Lord Jesus Christ. Therefore, our Lord Jesus Christ said, "And I will do whatever you ask in My NAME, (Jesus Christ), so, the Father will be glorified "in" the Son. (Jesus Christ).

Whatever you need to glorify our GOD the Father, ask of HIM in spiritual prayer in the NAME of our Lord Jesus Christ without a doubt.

- **James 1:6-8 (NIV)**
  6 But when you ask, you must believe and not doubt, because the one who doubts is like a wave of the sea, blown and tossed by the wind. 7 That person should not expect to receive anything from the LORD. (GOD the Father) 8 Such a person is Double-Minded and unstable in all they do.

And when you pray in Spirit to ask our GOD the Father in the NAME of our Lord "Jesus Christ," then our GOD the Father will do it for you. To either One you ask of, without a doubt, in the NAME of our Lord Jesus Christ, to glorify our GOD the Father, it will be done by the power of our GOD the Father and through our Lord Jesus Christ.

- **James 1:27 (NIV)**
  27 Religion that GOD our Father accepts as pure and faultless is this: to look after orphans and widows in their distress and to keep oneself from being polluted by the World.

———

Here is the Testimony of our GOD the Father that you may share with everyone to test their Spirit for Truth, in hopes that they believe it to be saved. Remember this Testimony by heart.

———

- **1 John 5:10-12 (NIV)**
  10 Whoever believes in the Son of GOD accepts this Testimony. Whoever does not believe GOD has made HIM out to be a liar, because they have not believed the Testimony GOD has given about HIS Son. 11 And this is the Testimony: **GOD has given us eternal Life, and this Life is in HIS Son. *12* Whoever has the Son has Life; whoever does not have the Son of GOD does not have Life**.

———

Now that we know the Word, we believe in it by doing what it says to do to show that we love our Lord Jesus Christ, the way our Lord Jesus Christ said to. Live in your Spirit, with the Holy Spirit, and obey the Word, with our GOD the Father in our Lord Jesus Christ, and with THEM living in you. You are never alone, and you will always have THEIR love living in you for eternal Life. All glory be to our GOD the Father through our Lord Jesus Christ, HIS only begotten Son.

Chapter 4: Believe and Follow Jesus Christ...

<u>And This Is Our Prayer:</u>

We pray in Spirit to give You glory, our GOD the Father, for Your Word of Truth that You gave to us as a gift for our sanctification through Your Son Jesus Christ. And by Your Testimony, we believe Your Son, our Lord Jesus Christ is the Way, the Truth, and the Life with the authority that You gave to Him for our salvation.

We ask for Your love to be in us forever, so that we may glorify You, our GOD the Father, and Your Son, our Lord Jesus Christ forever. We pray to ask You in the NAME of Your Son, our Lord Jesus Christ.

Chapter 5: The Holy Spirit with You Forever

John 14:15-31 NIV

15 "If you love Me, keep My commands." (Jesus Christ)

16 And I will ask the Father, and He will give you another Advocate (Holy Spirit) To help you and be with you forever —

17 the Spirit of Truth (Holy Spirit). The World cannot accept Him, because it neither sees Him nor knows Him. But you know Him, for He lives with you and will be in you.

18 I will not leave you as Orphans; I will come to you.

19 Before long, the World will not see Me anymore (Jesus Christ), but you will see Me. Because I live, you also will live.

20 On that day you will realize that I am in My Father, and you are in Me, and I am in you. (complete unity)

21 Whoever has My commands and keeps them is the one who loves Me. The one who loves Me will be loved by My Father, and I too will love them and show Myself to them.

22 Then Judas (not Judas Iscariot) said, "But, Lord, why do You intend to show Yourself to us and not to the World?"

23 Jesus replied, "Anyone who loves Me will obey My teaching. My Father will love them, and We (GOD the Father and Jesus Christ) will come to them and make our home with them.

Chapter 5: The Holy Spirit with You Forever

24 Anyone who does not love Me will not obey My teaching. These Words you hear are not My own; they belong to the Father who sent Me."

25 All this I have spoken while still with you.

26 But the Advocate, the Holy Spirit, whom the Father will send in My NAME, (Jesus Christ) will teach you all things and will remind you of everything I have said to you.

27 Peace I leave with you; My peace, I give you. I do not give to you as the World gives. Do not let your hearts be troubled and do not be afraid.

28 "You heard Me say, 'I am going away and I am coming back to you.' If you Loved Me, you would be glad that I am going to the Father, for the Father is greater than I.

29 I have told you now before it happens, so that when it does happen you will believe.

30 I will not say much more to you, for the prince of this World (Satan) is coming. He has no hold over Me,

31 but he (Satan) comes so that the World may learn that I love the Father and do exactly what My Father has commanded Me. Come now; let us leave.

❖ Notice:

Our Lord Jesus Christ said that He will ask our GOD the Father to send us His Holy Spirit to live within us, and He will be in us forever if we keep His commands. We must maintain our faith in the Word of Truth by learning and then practice living by it, by doing what the Word says to do while living in our personal Spirit and being guided by the Holy Spirit of our GOD the Father that is with us forever. And the Spirit of our Lord Jesus Christ is also living in us and tells the Holy Spirit what to tell us to say or do.

The Holy Spirit will help us reject immorality and reject any emotional habits such as lust and anxiety or influences that may lead us to sinful acts.

───

- **Romans 16:17-18 (NIV)**
  17 I urge you, Brothers and Sisters, to watch out for those who cause divisions and put obstacles in your way that are contrary to the teaching you have learned. Keep away from them. 18 For such people are not serving our Lord Christ, but their own appetites. By smooth talk and flattery they deceive the minds of naive people.

───

They are your enemies that you must resist and reject with all your mind, your soul, and your heart, in the NAME of our Lord Jesus Christ and He will help you because He loves you. And our Lord Jesus Christ will show Himself to you because you believe in Him and keep His commands. And because you love Him and He wants you to know that He is Always with you, that is why He will show Himself to you. He will show you that He is with you and helping you stay faithful. He will show Himself to you in many ways. And you will know it is Him by His love that you can feel in you because He is living in you.

Keep in mind, that you have your own "personal Spirit" that is you living in your Body-Temple, who are you since our GOD the Father created your Spirit and knew your Spirit first, and He formed you into your biological mother before you were born into your flesh. The flesh of your Body-Temple is dead without your Spirit living in it.

By the Word of our GOD the Father, our bodies of flesh are not meant to be everlasting. And at some point, in our lives, our Spirit will leave our Body-Temple and be raised up to be transformed into an imperishable

Chapter 5: The Holy Spirit with You Forever

Spirit-Body that will be able to live in the Realm of the Spirit and see the glory of our Lord Jesus Christ at His Throne in Heaven where He is. He prayed to our GOD the Father for this in His last hour, before He was Crucified. We will appear with Him to be presented Holy in the Holy presence of our GOD the Father.

His will is to do the will of our GOD the Father and give eternal Life to anyone who accepts Him in themselves and follows His commands while living in the Spirit in their Body-Temple on Earth. That is why we must repent our sins to live Holy in Spirit now.

Our Lord Jesus Christ is Spirit. Our GOD the Father made Him imperishable Spirit again after raising Him from the dead. He will do the same for us because no one can stand in the presence of our GOD the Father unless they are made imperishable first, or they will die from His immense power. And, with your Spirit, He formed you in the womb of your biological Mother to be born a living Soul in the flesh, by putting your Spirit into your flesh. That is a true miracle. Your Spirit is you, that will be awakened to eternal Life after you live in complete unity first in your Body-Temple, which is your appointed time to Decide and then prove your love for our Lord Jesus Christ, by keeping His commands. And that is believing while living in the Spirit by the New Covenant of our GOD the Father.

We must submit and commit ourselves to our GOD the Father, who is our eternal creator. And we submit and commit ourselves to Him through our Lord Jesus Christ, just as our GOD the Father has commanded us to do, by His own Grand Plan to reconcile with us on Earth, in Heaven, and Under Earth back to Himself. This is why He chose to give us a New Covenant for us to have and believe in by His Testimony. This is the Testimony of our GOD the Father about our Lord Jesus Christ.

―――

(The Testimony of our GOD the Father)

- **1 John 5:11-12 (NIV)**
  11 And this is the Testimony: **GOD has given us eternal Life, and this Life is in HIS Son.** *12* **Whoever has the Son has Life; whoever does not have the Son of GOD, does not have Life.**

- **Colossians 1:18-20 (NIV)**
  18 And He (Jesus Christ) *is the head of the Body, the Church; He is the beginning and the Firstborn from among the dead, so that in everything He might have the supremacy. 19 For GOD was pleased to have all His fullness dwell in Him, 20 and through Him* (Jesus Christ) *to reconcile to Himself all things,* (GOD the Father) *whether things on Earth or things in Heaven, by making peace through His blood shed on the cross.*

- **Jeremiah 1:5 (NIV)**
  5 "Before I formed you in the womb I knew you, before you were born I set you apart; I appointed you as a prophet to the Nations."

We must submit ourselves by our faith, and commit our Spirit by our deeds, to our GOD the Father through our Lord Jesus Christ. By our own free will, we must act on that Decision for eternal Life, to be guided by His Holy Spirit while living in the Spirit in our Body-Temple. That is living in complete unity with THEM.

Once you are committed to the Decision to follow the Holy Spirit as your spiritual guide, you must always follow His guidance to stay on the path He tells you so you do not get lost again and lose your life. With His Holy Spirit guiding you from within you, do not fear any evil as you are

Chapter 5: The Holy Spirit with You Forever

walking through the valley of death on Earth. Because all are condemned on Earth and living in vain for sin to their death without having our Lord Jesus Christ and the Holy Spirit of our GOD the Father helping us and giving life to us. He will guide you all the way through this lifetime on Earth and into the next lifetime of your imperishable Spirit in Heaven.

We plan in our heart where we want to go, but it is our GOD the Father that will make the Choices and establish each step we must take to have a strong foothold on His path of righteousness that leads to His presence in Heaven. We must remember, we are no longer making our own Choices of what to say or do, in word or deed without the guidance of His Holy Spirit. You must listen to what our Lord Jesus Christ says to the Holy Spirit, your guide, and do what He says to do and say to stay on the path. Listen for the Choice He tells you to take or you may be lost in corruption and die. Stay in complete unity by being guided by His Holy Spirit for eternal Life and to remain protected from evil.

The Seal of our GOD the Father is His Holy Spirit that He sends into you, that comes out from our GOD the Father, in the NAME of our Lord Jesus Christ and into you because He asked for that from our GOD the Father for you, to help guide you through your life now. The Holy Spirit will live with your Spirit in your Body-Temple to guide your Spirit and help you learn how to keep living in the Spirit by practicing living in the Word of our Lord Jesus Christ now. The written Word in the New Testament is our instruction of what we must do and not do, just as our Lord Jesus Christ lived as an example of how to conduct ourselves to please our GOD the Father. And we have the Testimony of the first chosen disciples that were enabled by the Holy Spirit to teach the Word, prophesy, perform miraculous healings, cast out unholy-spirits, and bless thousands of believers by baptizing them in the NAME of Jesus Christ our Lord, so they may also receive the Holy Spirit of our GOD the Father in themselves for eternal Life.

Exactly how our Lord Jesus Christ had commanded them to do, we are expected to do if and when we are enabled by the Holy Spirit of our GOD the Father. Anything we do in word or deed we must do by praying in Spirit and giving thanks to our GOD the Father, through and in the NAME of our Lord Jesus Christ. That includes baptizing in the NAME of Jesus Christ our Lord for every disciple to receive the Holy Spirit of our GOD the Father into their Body-Temple now. Baptizing is receiving our GOD the Father in Spirit by His Seal which is His Holy Spirit, and also the Spirit of our Lord Jesus Christ to become One with our personal Spirit, living in complete unity with THEM within our Body-Temple on Earth.

We must listen to the Holy Spirit at all times, through Him we receive many blessings and gifts from our GOD the Father through our Lord Jesus Christ by the help of the Holy Spirit guiding us at all times. The Holy Spirit will give and show you what Choices to take, because your Choice of words or deeds will be Chosen for you to keep you and your loved ones safe, while you learn to be living in the Spirit, to keep you on the narrow path of righteousness in this lifetime now serving our GOD the Father on Earth. He will tell you exactly what our Lord Jesus Christ is wanting you to do or say at the right time and place to bring glory to our GOD the Father.

Pray and ask our GOD the Father in the NAME of our Lord Jesus Christ while in spiritual prayer, of what to say or do, in word or deed, while giving thanks to our GOD the Father. You must no longer do or say anything, without asking for His Blessings in the NAME of our Lord Jesus Christ, while giving thanks to our GOD the Father in Spirit prayer. This is how we are to follow the guidance of His Holy Spirit: As a Servant to our GOD the Father in the NAME of His Son, our Lord Jesus Christ while keeping His commands in the Word.

Every path leads to death, except the one narrow path of eternal Life that leads to our GOD the Father. That is having our Lord Jesus Christ living in you and helping you with the guidance of the Holy Spirit speaking from your heart to you. Protect your heart at all times because everything from you, in word or deed, flows out from your heart. Listening to the Holy Spirit in you and to be living in complete unity with our Lord Jesus

Chapter 5: The Holy Spirit with You Forever

Christ is the way to righteousness and eternal Life with Him, as you live Holy now in your Body-Temple. You may have in your heart the desire to go somewhere or do something, but our GOD the Father makes your Choices and establishes every step for you to take on your journey by the guidance of His Holy Spirit in you.

- **Proverbs 16:9 (NIV)**
    9 In their hearts humans plan their course, but the LORD establishes their steps. ~ (GOD the Father)

Not everyone that says they have our Lord Jesus Christ actually have Him. You will know them by their deeds. They do not follow His commands, and they do not truly believe in Him, to know Him, and to have Him in themselves. Those are the foolish ones that stand condemned in their body, awaiting the execution of their personal Spirit on the Last Day along with the demons and Satan. They are all condemned and existing, without eternal Life living in them and doomed to destruction after they are Judged and see Shame on Judgement Day with their sin in themselves.

To believe the Testimony of our GOD the Father concerning our Lord Jesus Christ is to accept His New Covenant of the Spirit and to know that we are not our own. We live and pray in worship to our GOD the Father in the Spirit and by the NAME of our Lord Jesus Christ. We belong to our GOD the Father now with the eternal Life of our Lord Jesus Christ in our Body-Temple living within us in Spirit.

This is the Word, and it is the Truth.

- **Colossians 3:1-4 (NIV)**
    1 Since, then, you have been raised with Christ, set your

hearts on things above, where Christ is seated at the Right Hand of GOD. 2 Set your minds on things above, not on Earthly things. 3 For you died, and your life is now hidden with Christ in GOD. 4 When Christ, who is your life, appears, then you also will appear with Him in glory.

―――

- ### 1 Corinthians 6:19-20 (NIV)
  19 Do you not know that your Bodies are Temples of the Holy Spirit, who is in you, whom you have received from GOD? You are not your own; 20 you were bought at a price. Therefore, honor GOD with your Bodies.

―――

You are a disciple of our Lord Jesus Christ in learning and practicing the Word. He is our Church, in which we live now, in the Holy Spirit and complete unity. Wake up every day and live in the Spirit as you give thanks to our GOD the Father in the NAME of our Lord Jesus Christ. Have faith in our almighty GOD the Father to walk your walk, on your appointed path, that our GOD the Father has established your steps, predestined and appointed for you. The same as He did before you for every disciple, the prophets, the Apostles, and our Lord Jesus Christ, who all committed their Spirit to our GOD the Father, the creator of us all.

―――

- ### Luke 23:46 (NIV)
  46 Jesus called out with a loud Voice "Father, into your hands I commit My Spirit." When He had said this, He breathed His last.

―――

It is our GOD the Father that sends the Holy Spirit out from Himself and into us, in the NAME of our Lord "Jesus Christ". Because our Lord Jesus

Chapter 5: The Holy Spirit with You Forever

Christ asked for that in prayer for Him to do that for us to help us. Our GOD the Father does this for us because He loves us for keeping the commands written in His Word and believing His Testimony, which also shows Him we accepted His Covenant of Spirit and love our Lord Jesus Christ, His Son. Our Lord Jesus Christ said, "if you love Me, you would be glad I'm going to the Father-" Then He tells us why: "for the Father is greater than I."

This is the Word, and it is the Truth.

Now our Lord Jesus Christ is glorified even more than ever before; because He has been given Authority over Heaven and Earth, and Under Earth and is sitting at the Right Hand of our GOD the Father in Heaven, atoning for us on our behalf for our sins we repent.

- Romans 8:27, 34 (NIV)

    27 And He who searches our Hearts knows the mind of the Spirit, because the Holy Spirit intercedes for GOD'S people in accordance with the will of GOD.

    34 ...Christ Jesus who died—more than that, who was raised to Life— is at the Right Hand of GOD and is also interceding for us.

Our Lord Jesus Christ said, "These Words you hear are not My own, they belong to the Father who sent Me." The Word of Truth belongs to our GOD the Father. It is the Word of Truth that we need to accept as the Truth and live by it. This is how you will know if you are accepting and keeping the Word:

- I John 2:3 (NIV)

    3 We know that we have come to know Him if we keep His commands.

- **James 1:21-22 (NIV)**

  21 Therefore, get rid of all moral filth and the evil that is so prevalent, and humbly accept the Word planted in you, which can save you. 22 Do not merely listen to the Word, and so deceive yourselves. Do what it Says.

"Learn the Word and **do what the Word says to do.**"

- **I John 2:3-6 (NIV)**

  3 We know that we have come to know Him if we keep His commands. 4 Whoever says, "I know Him," but does not do what He commands is a liar, and the Truth is not in that person. 5 But if anyone obeys His Word, love for GOD is truly made complete in them. This is how we know we are in Him: 6 Whoever claims to live in Him lives as Jesus did.

That is how you know if you are keeping the Word and living by the Word of GOD the Father so you will not have doubts in you. Our Lord Jesus Christ mentioned, "the prince of this World;" He was referring to Satan. Satan was still in Judas and was on his way to His location with a group to arrest our Lord Jesus Christ. Remember this: the prince of this World (Satan) has no power over our Lord Jesus Christ. And our Lord Jesus Christ said, "Satan now stands condemned," meaning the Judgement stands now, that his spirit is condemned and is going to be destroyed at the appointed time. The demons know they also have their appointed time to be executed after Judgement, and that our Lord Jesus Christ is the Son of our GOD the Father that will do it. Especially since He was there, at that time in Heaven, and saw them get cast down to Earth from out of Heaven.

Chapter 5: The Holy Spirit with You Forever

All those that Decide to reject our Lord Jesus Christ, have more love for living with their desire of the sin in their flesh. They will all see Shame and Judgement expedited when their Spirit appears at the judgment seat of our Lord Jesus Christ. And their Spirit will be destroyed, according to their condemnation for keeping sin, when they are Judged at their appointed time.

Being Judged for sin only means one's condemned Spirit being executed to death, for the Evil and sin one kept living with and committing in one's body. If you believe and know our Lord Jesus Christ, and you know the Testimony of our GOD the Father concerning Him, you will know the Truth in the Word.

This is the Word, and it is the Truth.

- ### Mathew 8:28-33 (NIV)
  28 When He (Jesus Christ) *arrived at the other side in the Region of the Gadarenes, two "demon-possessed men" coming from the tombs met Him. They were so violent that no one could pass that way. 29 "What do You want with us, Son of GOD?" they shouted. "Have You come here to torture us before the appointed time?" 30 Some distance from them a large herd of pigs was feeding. 31 The demons begged Jesus, "If You drive us out, send us into the herd of pigs." 32 He (Jesus Christ) said to them, "Go!" So, they came out and went into the pigs, and the whole herd rushed down the steep bank into the lake and died in the water. 33 Those tending the pigs ran off, went into the town and reported all this, including what had happened to the demon-possessed men.*

Be as fearless as our Lord Jesus Christ is fearless; as He is living fearless in us with the Holy Spirit, just as our GOD the Father is living in our Lord Jesus Christ. No one can stand against THEM living in you.

———

- ### 1 Corinthians 11:3 (NIV)
  3 But I want you to realize that the Head of every Man is Christ, and the Head of the Woman is Man, and the Head of Christ is GOD.

———

That is why it is often written for (You) in scripture: (You) have faith in our GOD the Father, (You) believe in our GOD the Father, (You) also believe in our Lord Jesus Christ. (You) do not let your Hearts be troubled, and (You) do not be afraid.

———

Be cautious of evil, but do not fear evil as (You) resist the evil of demons that will try to turn you against our Lord Jesus Christ, and our GOD the Father, and turn you against yourself for living by the Word. Whenever evil ones lie to you, reproach their lies with the Word of Truth that you learned. Reject the thoughts of any lie out of your mind, in the NAME of our Lord Jesus Christ, as soon as you hear it, or if it crosses your mind.

Reject any thoughts that may lead you into sin. Just say, "I reject that thought in the NAME of Jesus Christ." If anyone dares to approach you with a lie, reproach them with the Word of Truth to protect your mind, which is Holy and belongs to our GOD the Father. Your Body-Temple of flesh can die; but no one can condemn your Spirit, which is you, living in your Body-Temple of flesh. No one can condemn you except by the authority of our GOD the Father, and that authority has been given to His Son. Our Lord Jesus Christ, who lives in us believers. Keep His commands because we love Him, and our Spirits have crossed over from death to eternal Life because He lives in us. And by living with THEM in you, your Spirit belongs to our GOD the Father for eternal Life.

Chapter 5: The Holy Spirit with You Forever

No one else has the power to destroy any Spirit that our GOD the Father created, not without the power of HIS authority. And our Lord Jesus Christ has been given that authority from our GOD the Father for the Last Day to use at His discretion. The Judgement Day of the wicked and non-believers. Do not be afraid, because our Lord Jesus Christ is already living with His life and love in you now; interceding on your behalf to our GOD the Father. Because we have already submitted and committed ourselves to our GOD the Father. We also accepted our Lord Jesus Christ as our Savior to live in unity with THEM in us, so we have no reason to fear the day we see our Lord Jesus Christ in His glory at His Throne where He is, that is our day for redemption. And our Lord Jesus Christ is ready to take us to our GOD the Father when it is our time that our GOD the Father has appointed for each of us.

With the Holy Spirit within us, there is no place found in us for any evil, or any demon that we can resist with the Word in the NAME of our Lord Jesus Christ anyway. And we will appear Holy in the presence of our GOD the Father with our Lord Jesus Christ. At that time the Holy Spirit will testify with your Spirit for you, to receive the Crown of eternal Life.

- **James 4**
   6 But He gives us more grace. That is why scripture says: "GOD opposes the proud, but shows favor to the humble." 7 Submit yourselves, then, to GOD. Resist the devil, and he will flee from you.

We now know there is complete unity with the Holy Spirit in us all. We, as believers of our Lord Jesus Christ are as One Holy Spirit family, Brothers and Sisters, Heirs to the Kingdom of our GOD the Father with our Lord Jesus Christ. Pay close attention to the Holy Spirit that guides you through your life from within you. He is speaking what our Lord Jesus Christ wants you to know. That is how you will know what to say and do. The Holy Spirit will speak to you in the scriptures, the Word, thoughts, dreams, memories, and feelings of urgency when it is time to take action. And He gives you signs to let you know that He did something for you to remind you that He is in you, so you will not doubt Him.

He will put you in the right place, at the right time, and help you speak the right words that you learned from the scriptures, by reminding you of the Word you learned. And He will warn you about troubles in your future so you can persevere through any problem that may cross your path. That is what will come your way living in the Spirit and having fellowship with the Holy Spirit in complete unity within you. Together, in complete unity, we will find every Brother and Sister who is bound and blinded by the lies of Satan. And we will help snatch them out from the fire of condemnation, to set them free with the Word of Truth and the guidance of His Holy Spirit in us which is sent down from our GOD the Father in Heaven through our Lord Jesus Christ. His Holy Spirit empowers us to do what is needed at the right time. And we will also be protected from the evil one, by the NAME of our Lord Jesus Christ, the NAME that we call on for them and their salvation.

The Holy Spirit in you protects everyone you love and pray for. By Having our Lord Jesus Christ in your heart, He will protect your children and your marriage because He knows your deepest desires with your loved ones, and lives in you to bring you all to Himself for the glory of our GOD the Father. And by our prayer in Spirit to glorify our GOD the Father, our Lord Jesus Christ will protect them by His NAME. With the Holy Spirit living in us we will keep the commands to Always Love Each Other on Earth as we will in Heaven.

And This Is Our Prayer:

We pray in Spirit to You, our GOD the Father, and we thank You for loving us by sending our Lord Jesus Christ to us with Your Word of Truth to sanctify our souls for our salvation now on Earth.

And we thank You for sending Your Holy Spirit, in the NAME of our Lord Jesus Christ to be living in us and helping us keep Your commands to meet your righteous requirement. We ask You to protect us with the NAME of our Lord Jesus Christ.

We ask You in the NAME of Your only begotten Son, our Lord Jesus Christ.

Chapter 6: *Remain in HIS Son Jesus Christ*

John 15:1-8 NIV

1 "I am the true Vine (Jesus Christ), and My Father is the Gardener.

2 HE cuts off every Branch in Me that bears no fruit, while every Branch that does bear fruit, HE prunes so that it will be even more fruitful.

3 You are already clean because of the Word I have spoken to you.

4 Remain in Me, as I also remain in you. No Branch can bear fruit by itself; it must remain in the Vine. Neither can you bear fruit unless you remain in Me.

5 "I am the Vine; you are the Branches. If you remain in Me and I in you, you will bear much fruit; apart from Me you can do nothing.

6 If you do not remain in Me, you are like a Branch that is thrown away and withers; such Branches are picked up, thrown into the fire and burned.

7 If you remain in Me and My Words remain in you, ask whatever you wish, and it will be done for you.

8 This is to My Father's glory, that you bear much fruit, showing yourselves to be My disciples.

Chapter 6: Remain in His Son Jesus Christ

❖ Notice:

Bear no fruit and be cut off by our GOD the Father; or be more fruitful by our GOD the Father directly pruning you, and caring for you, as you remain attached to our Lord Jesus Christ in unity. Remaining in our Lord Jesus Christ is part of being in complete unity. Living with the Holy Spirit and our Lord Jesus Christ in you, as One in spiritual unity is part of complete unity.

Complete unity is accepting the Spirit of our Lord Jesus Christ and the baptism of the Holy Spirit from our GOD the Father, in the NAME of our Lord Jesus Christ. And that is by submitting and committing your Spirit to reconcile with our GOD the Father in the NAME of HIS Son, Jesus Christ, by giving thanks to our GOD the Father in spiritual prayer and by asking of HIM in the NAME of our Lord Jesus Christ, to send HIS Holy Spirit into you, and by accepting the Spirit of our Lord Jesus Christ, "The Word of Life", into you. And once you have done this, you must then practice living by the message in the Word to keep HIS commands, while you remain living in your personal Spirit with THEM as THEY remain in you for complete unity. Now you are a legitimate and Holy Child of GOD worshipping in the Spirit as One with Them.

Bear fruit is learning the Word, having faith, and doing the deeds that please our GOD the Father, by living in the Spirit to help others reconcile with our GOD the Father through our Lord Jesus Christ, and to teach others the Gospel and the message in the Word; so, they may get to know our GOD the Father and our Lord Jesus Christ, to believe in THEM for eternal Life. Then our Lord Jesus Christ will do what He needs to do for them to bring them closer to our GOD the Father, to know HIM too. That is having our Lord Jesus Christ helping you from within you to do what only He can do with the Power of Life in Him.

It is truly a miracle when someone gets saved, not by us, but by our Lord Jesus Christ working through the Holy Spirit to help them become sanctified and then anointed with the Holy Spirit and the Spirit of our

Lord Jesus Christ. This is the "deed" our GOD the Father expects of all believers to do to remain in complete unity with THEM. Those who do not live their lives helping others reconcile to our GOD the Father through our Lord Jesus Christ will be cut off from eternal Life for denying HIM and HIS Son before others.

To live your life now without sharing the New Covenant and the Testimony of our GOD the Father with others is, weak in faith, cowardly, and lack of commitment to our GOD the Father. Therefore, those that do not bear fruit, can surely expect to be disowned by our Lord Jesus Christ, and be cut off by our GOD the Father, then destroyed for their condemnation in sin for not obeying the command to Always Love Each Other and help them learn to believe in the New Covenant of our GOD the Father concerning our Lord Jesus Christ.

Do not take "believing" lightly, having the courage to say that you believe is not faith. Faith is proven by action, by doing what you know is right, and by having what you believe written in your heart. And since everything you believe in you flows from your heart, wanting to do the righteous things taught in the Word is believing in our Lord Jesus Christ when you practice doing what is written in the Word that you learned. It takes love for righteousness in the Word and all the courage you have to do the things it says to do while you are living by the Spirit.

Thinking you believe in a higher power is not believing and saying you believe in a higher power is not believing in the living GOD. Knowing our GOD the Father by HIS Testimony concerning HIS Son, our Lord Jesus Christ and following the commands in HIS written Word, by doing what it says to do, and believing in your Heart and saying what the Word says to is showing that you love THEM both when you proclaim with your mouth that Jesus Christ is your Lord, then you have eternal Life.

You must be willing to die for believing in our Lord Jesus Christ and live by it on Earth until your Body-Temple dies. That is how we show that we love our Lord Jesus Christ in complete unity and deserve to have eternal Life. Be bold and enthusiastic in your faith having our Lord Jesus

Chapter 6: Remain in His Son Jesus Christ

Christ within you as One, because there are many others that are being called to Him and want to know how to have Him in themselves. And it's up to believers to step up and keep up with the guidance of the Holy Spirit to teach them the Truth.

Sharing this Gospel and the Word of Truth in these scriptures is enough to help everyone with their Decision to believe and accept the New Covenant and the Testimony of our GOD the Father to have eternal Life and remain in our Lord Jesus Christ.

- **James 2:26 (NIV)**
  26 As the body without the Spirit is dead, so faith without deeds is dead.

- **Galatians 6:7-8 (NIV)**
  7 Do not be deceived: GOD cannot be mocked. A man reaps what he sows. 8.... whoever sows to please the Spirit, from the Spirit will reap eternal Life.

- **Philippians 1:27 (NIV)**
  27 Whatever happens, conduct yourselves in a manner worthy of the Gospel of Christ.... you stand firm in the One Spirit, striving together as One for the faith of the Gospel without being frightened in any way by those who oppose you. This is a sign to them that they will be destroyed, but that you will be saved, and that by GOD.

GOD the Father will make your path straight. Expect to be pruned, trimmed, moved, cleaned, nourished, nurtured, and tempered into a position of learning to bear even more Fruit. Be humble in nature and bold in speaking the Word while living in the Spirit to help others learn the message in the Word and keep the commands including to Always Love Each Other. You are working to glorify our GOD the Father by helping to reconcile all those who are being called to HIM. Remember, we are responsible for helping everyone who wants to turn to our Lord Jesus Christ and accepting them as they are with all their sin, and all their sinful habits, to teach them that they must repent to our God the Father in the NAME of HIS Son Jesus.

The sin that you repent for your salvation is between you and our Lord Jesus Christ because only He can forgive you to sanctify your Soul to make you a Holy Child of our GOD the Father. And HE, our GOD the Father, wants all to turn to HIM through HIS Son Jesus Christ. We are not to learn about their sin and shame in others; but to teach them the Testimony of our GOD the Father concerning HIS Son and how to believe in HIM and our Lord Jesus Christ, to know THEM and accept THEM and live in complete unity with THEM, so they may turn away from sin and be saved by our Lord Jesus Christ for eternal Life. Because only by knowing and having a personal Spirit relationship with THEM can we be saved.

- **James 1:27 (NIV)**
    27 Religion that GOD our Father accepts as pure and faultless is this: To look after orphans and widows in their distress, and to keep oneself from being polluted by the World.

Anyone that lacks a strong vessel, as a leader in their household to help them keep the Word, is also like an orphan or widow in distress. And we are all like a child to our GOD the Father learning how to walk and talk in the Word and keep the commands. We are HIS Children, as Brothers

Chapter 6: Remain in His Son Jesus Christ

and Sisters in our Lord Jesus Christ, and we all must be brought up to become mature in HIS Word. Our inheritance from HIM is eternal Life in HIS Kingdom. Learn to keep living by HIS Word to temper your faith to become stronger.

- **Mathew 19:14 (NIV)**
  14 Jesus said, "Let the little children come to Me, and do not hinder them, for the Kingdom of Heaven belongs to such as these."

It is our responsibility to share whatever gift we have been blessed with, to help them learn the Word of Truth to glorify our GOD the Father. Warn them of the danger of sin, in hopes that they don't turn to a life of sin and lose their eternal Life. You will be held accountable for their life, if you fail to warn them, then you both will lose your life. If you warn them, you will not lose your life. And if they don't turn to sin because they took your warning, you and they will be blessed by our GOD the Father.

When living in unity with our Lord Jesus Christ and the Holy Spirit, we are compelled to Preach the Gospel in the Word. You will be told to say or do something for another to help them turn and focus their hearts and minds on our Lord Jesus Christ. And when you do, make sure to glorify our GOD the Father in everything you do for them, to bring them closer

to our GOD the Father in the NAME of our Lord Jesus Christ. And by your praying in Spirit, our GOD the Father will come closer to them.

- **Colossians 3:1-4 (NIV)**
  1 Since, then, you have been raised with Christ, set your hearts on things above, where Christ is, seated at the Right Hand of GOD. 2 Set your minds on things above, not on Earthly things. 3 For you died, and Your Life is now hidden with Christ in GOD. 4 When Christ, who is your Life, appears, then you also

will appear with Him in glory.

- **Colossians 3:17 (NIV)**
  17 And whatever you do, whether in word or deed, do it all in the NAME of the Lord Jesus, giving thanks to GOD the Father through Him. ~ (Jesus Christ)

Our deeds are to glorify our GOD the Father in the NAME of HIS Son Jesus Christ and continue to make THEM known to all the World by sharing the message in the Word of Truth. For that, we have a promised reward at our redemption. Our prize is the Crown of Eternal Life that our GOD the Father gives us through the Spirit of Life and the authority that HE put in HIS Son, our Lord Jesus Christ. We must know THEM now and have our Lord Jesus Christ living in us now for eternal Life.

All those that refuse to have our Lord Jesus Christ living in them now, are "nothing" without Him. They are living in vain and have no eternal Life in them now or later. They are condemned now for the sin in them because they refuse to believe in the Testimony of our GOD the Father. And they have no eternal Life now or after they die in their flesh because their spirit will be taken to the Judgement Seat of our Lord Jesus Christ to be executed out of existence. Any good they ever did will not be remembered because they denounced our Lord Jesus Christ by their actions, the same as the angels that fell from grace in Heaven and were cast out of Heaven and Hurled down to Earth until the last day where they will see their doom and destruction at the Last Day. They all stand condemned now, the same as Satan stands condemned now. The same as Judas Iscariot who is doomed to destruction for denouncing our Lord Jesus Christ by his actions. All the condemned are awaiting the execution of their spirit in the same place that the existence of Death itself will be destroyed and will no longer exist. That is the fate of this World, Hades, Sheol, and Death, and whatever is part of the World and how all evil ones will be discarded.

Chapter 6: Remain in His Son Jesus Christ

The spirits of those who refuse to live with our Lord Jesus Christ will all be consigned to the Lake of Fire for their Second Death. They are living in vain for nothing; because on the Last Day they will all be Raised up to see, hear, and be taken to that place prepared for the wicked and non-believers for their Final Judgement to be executed as it is written in the Word of Truth. Their Spirits are going to be consigned to the Lake of Fire, at their Appointed Time to be destroyed in the Second Death, and then destroyed so they no longer pose a threat to the Children of our GOD the Father forever. Only believers that live with our Lord Jesus Christ now will enter the New Kingdom of GOD on the New World conjoined with a New Heaven with eternal Life, coexisting together with our GOD the Father.

- **1 Corinthians 9:16-18 (NIV)**

  16 For when I preach the Gospel, I cannot boast, since I am compelled to preach. Woe to me "if I do not preach the Gospel!" 17 If I preach voluntarily, I have a reward; if not voluntarily, I am simply discharging the trust committed to me. 18 What then is my reward? Just this: that in preaching the gospel I may offer it free of charge, and so not make full use of my rights as a Preacher of the gospel.

- **1 Corinthians 9:22-23 (NIV)**

  22 To the weak I became weak, to win the weak. I have become all things to all people so that by all possible means I might save some. 23 I do all this for the sake of the Gospel, that I may share in its blessings.

- **1 Corinthians 9:26-27 (NIV)**

  26 Therefore I do not run like someone running aimlessly; I do not fight like a boxer beating the air. 27 No, I strike a blow to my body and make it my slave so that after I have preached to others, I myself will not be disqualified for the prize.

Our Lord Jesus Christ said, "You are already clean because of the Word I have spoken to you." We are sanctified and cleaned from hearing and believing the message in the Word that our Lord Jesus Christ taught us, which is now written in the New Testament of the Bible. But you still need to have the Son, our Lord Jesus Christ living in you to have eternal Life.

As believers we have left behind living by the desires of our 'flesh of death', that we inherited at birth with the wrath of our GOD the Father that was set against it because of the transgression of the first two Humans created. We left that way of living by the desires of the flesh because we Decided to accept HIS Choice for us to live in our Spirit with HIS Holy Spirit and the Spirit of our Lord Jesus Christ living in us in complete unity without sin.

The Choice for us to have eternal Life is not made by us. Our GOD the Father has mercy on us and "HE made the Choice for us to have eternal Life". And HE made eternal Life in HIS Son for us to believe in HIMSELF and HIS Son, with the Innocent Blood Sacrifice He spilled to cleanse us from the sin that we repent as believers. If you believe Him in your Heart and proclaim with your Mouth, "Jesus Christ is your Lord living in you," Then you have our Lord Jesus Christ in you, and the Life in Him gives you eternal Life if you keep His commands. And all believers, believe in the Testimony of our GOD the Father concerning our Lord Jesus Christ. It is only "our Decision" to gracefully accept the gift of eternal Life that our GOD the Father willfully desires to give us all.

Those who refuse to have the gift of Life, which is in our Lord Jesus Christ, are already condemned and awaiting the Second Death. Unless someone can help them change their way of living to learn the Truth in the Word, that we must live in our Spirit to be guided by the Holy Spirit of our GOD the Father. They must first understand and believe in the

Chapter 6: Remain in His Son Jesus Christ

Word of Truth to be sanctified. Then they must commit to accept living in their Spirit and go to our Lord Jesus Christ for eternal Life while giving thanks to our GOD the Father by praying in Spirit.

The only way to eternal Life is through having the Spirit of our Lord Jesus Christ living in our heart now, in our Body-Temple, with the Holy Spirit of our GOD the Father all living in us as One in complete unity. We are guided by HIS Holy Spirit in everything we say and do. We will do nothing without the blessings of our GOD the Father through our Lord Jesus Christ.

This is the Word, and it is the Truth.

Our Lord Jesus Christ teaches the message in the Word using simple language, so there is no confusion when learning the Truth to believe in Him. He proves and reproves that the Word is the Truth in many ways by using scriptures, so we can also prove and reprove His Testimony, which includes the Testimony of our GOD the Father that sent Him to us for our salvation from the penalty of sin.

- ### Philippians 2:1-11 (NIV)

    1 Therefore if you have any encouragement from being united with Christ, if any comfort from His love, if any common sharing in the Spirit, if any tenderness and compassion, 2 then make my joy complete by being like-minded, having the same love, being One in Spirit and of One mind. 3 Do nothing out of selfish ambition or vain conceit. Rather, in humility value others above yourselves, 4 not looking to your own interests but each of you to the interests of the others. 5 In your relationships with one another, have the same mindset as Christ Jesus: 6 who being in very nature GOD, did not consider equality with GOD something to be used to His own advantage; 7 rather, He made Himself nothing by taking the very nature of a

Servant being made in Human likeness, 8 and being found in appearance as a Man, (Son of Man) He humbled Himself by becoming obedient to death even death on a cross! 9 Therefore, GOD exalted Him to the Highest Place and gave Him the NAME that is above every Name, 10 that at the NAME of Jesus every knee should bow in Heaven and on Earth and Under the Earth, 11 and every tongue acknowledge that Jesus Christ is Lord, to the glory of GOD, the Father.

By being this way, of taking the mindset of our Lord Jesus Christ, we will not doubt our intentions when we put the interest of others first. As it is, the double-minded person is the one who has doubts and who can't commit to living their life now by the Truth, and therefore will not believe in it to meet the righteous requirement to stand in the presence of our GOD the Father. That is how and why they will remain standing condemned. They ignore the Word and continue to believe in self-righteousness and live the way they want to in selfish ambition, which is living sanctimoniously. And that is completely the opposite of being humble. Sanctimonious one's thinking is, not committing to accept living with the help of our Lord Jesus Christ in all that they do.

Remember what our Lord Jesus Christ explained, that without His help we have no part in Him, as He explained to the Apostle Simon Peter. Without His help by accepting Him, we have no life now and stand condemned now and forever; or by following His commands with His help and by accepting Him in unity we have eternal Life now. Keep in mind, no one can be reconciled to our GOD the Father and enter eternal Life without first believing in the Testimony of our GOD the Father, to have a spiritual relationship with our Lord Jesus Christ with His life in themselves.

No one can have our Lord Jesus Christ without believing in doing exactly what He told us to do and how to remain in Him. He is our Life

Chapter 6: Remain in His Son Jesus Christ

source living within us as our GOD the Father explains in HIS Testimony. That is our New Covenant, and our Lord Jesus Christ fulfills the New Covenant in us, with every person that believes in Him and our GOD the Father now. That is how we take part in Him as One to stand Holy with each other in complete unity with THEM for eternal Life.

Following His commands in the Word that He teaches us, is the way we show that we love Him and that we are His disciples willing to stand Holy now. You must have our Lord Jesus Christ and His Spirit of Life dwelling in you now, for the crossing over from death to eternal Life. And the Holy Spirit of our GOD the Father will help you stay connected to our Lord Jesus Christ to stand Holy and bear more fruit at this appointed time with the help of our GOD the Father making us more fruitful in our Holy Body-Temple with THEM.

This is the Word, and it is the Truth.

- **1 John 5:10-12 (NIV)**

   10 Whoever believes in the Son of GOD accepts this Testimony. Whoever does not believe GOD has made HIM out to be a liar, because they have not believed the Testimony GOD has given about HIS Son. 11 And this is the Testimony: ***GOD has given us eternal Life, and this Life is in HIS Son. 12 Whoever has the Son has Life; Whoever does not have the Son of GOD does not have Life.***

Our Lord Jesus Christ spoke to the ones who taught the scriptures to the people at that time and explained what it means to believe in the Word of our GOD the Father. The things that they learned was in their minds to ponder, but they didn't have it written in their hearts to be compelled by what they believe in their hearts to do what it says to do and go to our Lord Jesus Christ for eternal Life. He is the Way, the Truth, and the Life in you and with you forever.

- **John 5:37-40 (NIV)**
  37 And the Father who sent Me has HIMSELF Testified concerning Me. (Jesus Christ) You have never heard HIS Voice nor seen HIS form, 38 nor does HIS Word dwell in you, for you do not believe the One HE sent. 39 You study the scriptures diligently because you think that in them you have eternal Life. These are the very scriptures that Testify about Me, 40 yet you refuse to come to Me to have Life.

We must stop listening to false prophets and lying preachers who mix the confusing and conflicting doctrine of the World into the scriptures to please their own appetites. Learn what our Lord Jesus Christ taught consistently and live by the Word of Truth. By believing in this Testimony of the Apostle John you are sanctified by the Truth, and by accepting to live by it you will have eternal Life. Don't let the confused words of others confuse you, especially when you know the Truth and have crossed over from death to eternal Life. We don't Judge ourselves and others as being unworthy to be forgiven. We are now sanctified and forgiven for all our sins and are now living without sin with our Lord Jesus Christ and His Life living in us.

We do not have to wait for the Judgement Day to find out if we are worthy to be saved; no one can be saved at the Judgement Seat without the Spirit of our Lord Jesus Christ and fellowship with the Holy Spirit of our GOD the Father living in their Body-Temple now and at our redemption when we are Raised up to the clouds to meet our Holy Ones that have been raised up from their graves first with our Lord Jesus Christ. Our GOD the Father makes us worthy of eternal Life now by the Choice that HE made for us with HIS New Covenant; at the moment when we first believe in HIS Testimony, and in HIS Son, The Word of Life, then

Chapter 6: Remain in His Son Jesus Christ

receive the Holy Spirit in us for eternal Life now. With that, all believers are living Holy without sin with the eternal Life in our Lord Jesus Christ who are both living in them now.

This is the Word, and it is the Truth.

———

And now that we believe in our Lord Jesus Christ with His message in the Word and that He has the authority and the Life in Him to forgive us and give us eternal Life, as we continue to mature in the Word to change our mind, our heart, and our habits, to do good deeds. And we may come to Him with all our sins in us to be forgiven and receive the promise of eternal Life, as we are told we must do by our GOD the Father in HIS Testimony about HIS Son, our Lord Jesus Christ. We have already passed over from death to eternal Life. Therefore, we will not see Judgement or Shame at the Judgement Seat, His Throne, because there is nothing left in us to be Judged by; when we already live in the Spirit, with the Life of our Lord Jesus Christ living in us and giving our Spirit eternal Life, right now, at this appointed time to prove we love THEM.

At the time we are Raised up, we will receive the Crown of Eternal Life, which is the Crown of Righteousness, and the Crown of Glory. That is why our Lord Jesus Christ told the Apostles, because I live, you will live. If you are not worthy of eternal Life, our Lord Jesus Christ will not dwell in you with your sin in you. Yet He said, no one will be turned away that comes to Him for Life so you can believe without a doubt that you can repent to Him and He will forgive you whatever you repent. So, it is true that you have been given free will, and you are aware that you stand condemned without our Lord Jesus Christ, and that no one has any excuse not to go to our Lord Jesus Christ for the gift of eternal Life.

Repent your sins now and give thanks by praying in Spirit to our GOD the Father now, in the NAME of HIS Son Jesus Christ for eternal Life. And everyone that Decides to remain without Him now, stands condemned now. Everyone that Decides to remain with Him now, has eternal Life now. The World has been put on notice by our GOD the Father through HIS Son Jesus Christ that we all stand condemned with the gift of Life ready for us to receive and cross over from death to eternal Life.

This is the Word, and it is the Truth.

- ### John 6:37-40 (NIV)
  37 All those the Father gives Me will come to Me, and whoever comes to Me I will never drive away. 38 For I have come down from Heaven not to do My will (Jesus Christ) but to do the will of HIM who sent Me. (GOD the Father) 39 And this is the will of HIM who sent Me, that: I shall lose none of all those HE has given Me, but raise them up at the Last Day. 40 For My Fathers' will is that everyone who looks to the Son and believes in Him shall have eternal Life, and I will raise them up at the Last Day."

The key word is believe, by doing what it says to do, not just knowing that is true. Even Satan knows the Word is the Truth, but Satan chooses not to do what it says to do", and he fools people into thinking that you don't have to "do what it says to do". That is a lie, from the Father of Lies, Satan. Some of the smartest people fall for that lie and will not accept to have our Lord Jesus Christ and His eternal Life in them, by refusing to accept to live by His commands.

Therefore, they will be cut off from eternal Life now by our GOD the Father, for not showing that they believe in HIS Son, our Lord Jesus Christ. Without having a relationship living in the Spirit with Him living in us, we do not have eternal Life. Believing in Him is also by doing what the Word says to do, and that is how we show our love for our Lord Jesus Christ and our GOD the Father. For that THEY will love us and remain in us as we remain in THEM, in complete unity because we are doing

Chapter 6: Remain in His Son Jesus Christ

HIS will as we suffer now for a little while, at this appointed time in our eternal Life, to keep all HIS Word in our heart and the commands written in it.

- ### John 14:21 (NIV)
  21 Whoever has My commands and keeps them is the one who loves Me. The one who loves Me will be loved by My Father, and I too love them and show Myself to them."

With Him living in us now, we have eternal Life while living in Spirit now. This is the message in the Word, and it is the Truth.

- ### John 5:22-24 (NIV)
  22 Moreover, the Father judges no one, but has entrusted all Judgement to the Son, 23 that all may honor the Son just as they honor the Father. Whoever does not honor the Son does not honor the Father, who sent Him. 24 **"Very truly I tell you**, *whoever hears My Word and believes HIM who sent Me has eternal Life and will not be judged" but has crossed over from death to Life.*

With our Lord Jesus Christ living in us, we feel His love in our hearts when He tells us something through the Holy Spirit or helps us to do something to glorify our GOD the Father. Seek to be always doing the will of our GOD the Father, and HE will make your heart feel at peace for living by the Word with our Lord Jesus Christ in you.

And This Is Our Prayer:

We pray in Spirit to ask You, our GOD the Father, to bless us and nurture us with everything we need to be sanctified by Your Word, so we can remain attached to Your Son, our Lord Jesus Christ. Without His help, we can do nothing, and we would be nothing. We ask You to make us more fruitful by the works of Your Hand so we may bring others to know You, our GOD the Father, and Your Son, our Lord Jesus Christ, for your blessing of eternal Life. We pray to ask of You, in the NAME of Your Son, our Lord Jesus Christ.

Chapter 7: Jesus Christ our Friend…keep His Commands

John 15: 9-17 NIV

9 "As the Father has loved Me, so have I loved you. Now remain in My love.

10 If you keep My commands, you will remain in My love, just as I have kept My Father's commands and remain in HIS love.

11 I have told you this so that My joy may be in you and that your joy may be complete.

12 My command is this: Love Each Other, as I have loved you.

13 Greater love has no one than this: to lay down one's life for one's friends.

14 You are My friends If you do what I command.

15 I no longer call you servants because a servant does not know his Master's business. Instead, I have called you friends, for everything that I learned from My Father I have made known to you.

16 You did not choose Me, but I chose you and appointed you so that you might go and bear fruit—Fruit that will last—And so that whatever you ask in My NAME the Father will give you.

17 This is My command: Love Each Other.

Chapter 7: Jesus Christ our Friend...

❖ Notice:

Our Lord Jesus Christ tells us the way He remained in the love of our GOD the Father. It is exactly how we will remain in the love of our Lord Jesus Christ and our GOD the Father. This is how, "keep His commands." And His New Command is for us to always love each other. Our Lord Jesus Christ has the most profound knowledge of every Word in all the written Law and more knowledge than anyone can imagine, because everything He learned, He learned from our GOD the Father. We must always practice doing what the Word of our Lord Jesus Christ says to do and say to the glory of our GOD the Father. Therefore, we must always practice living by the New Command to Always Love Each Other.

Although we don't know the exact age of the Earth, Solar system, or the Universe we reside in, but starting in the billions of years is a good start in our minds if you want to understand what our Lord Jesus Christ meant when He said that He was before the Earth was made, or anything was made. Then when our GOD the Father sent Him from Heaven to Earth to be a Sin Offering to sacrifice for our Sins, He humbled Himself into that which is nothing, which is a Human Servant that is made in Human Likeness. So, He could do nothing and say nothing without our GOD the Father showing and telling Him what to say and do by HIS commands. We must do the same as the example our Lord Jesus Christ has done because that is who we are to become like, that is exactly what we are made to be, Servants in Human Likeness to our GOD the Father, and nothing without the power of our GOD the Father working through our Lord Jesus Christ living in us.

No one on Earth has anything to boast about without having our Lord Jesus Christ because only He has been exalted to the Highest Position on the Right Hand of our GOD the Father who glorified HIS Son, Our Lord Jesus Christ, with the power of Life and Authority over all creation. No one becomes anything or gets anything without asking for it in spiritual prayer from our GOD the Father through acknowledging HIS Son by His NAME as our Lord Jesus Christ. Only then will HE hear our prayer in Spirit worship, and only then we will receive help from the power of our GOD the Father through the help of our Lord Jesus Christ.

Therefore, our Lord Jesus Christ said, that the Son can do nothing on His own, He can only do what He sees and hears what our GOD the Father shows Him what He must say and do. He has been given the authority over all things to help us and make us become Holy Children of our GOD the Father. That is exactly what He learned and then taught us to do and say as it is written in the Word of Truth.

- ### John 5:19-20 (NIV)
    *<u>19</u> Jesus gave them this answer: "**Very truly I tell you**, the Son can do nothing by Himself; He can only do what He sees HIS Father doing, because whatever the Father does the Son also does. <u>20</u> For the Father loves the Son and shows Him all HE does. Yes, and HE will show Him even greater works than these, "So that you will be amazed."*

- ### John 5:30 (NIV)
    <u>30</u> By Myself I can do nothing; (Jesus Christ) *I Judge only as I hear, and My Judgement is just, for I seek not to please Myself, but HIM* (GOD the Father) *who sent Me.* ~ (Jesus Christ)

Keep in mind the books of the New Testament containing the Gospel, were not written when our Lord Jesus Christ walked in Human Likeness because it was about His Life. There was only the Old Testament that contained prophecies concerning the coming of our Lord Jesus Christ and what He would do on Earth to help reconcile Humanity with our GOD the Father. Yet, with all the history, knowledge, and wisdom written in the scriptures, He still gave us a New Command to always

Chapter 7: Jesus Christ our Friend...

keep in our hearts and to always practice living by, to Always Love Each Other. He reiterated it many times in different phrases to express to us exactly how important it is to keep the New Command. If we did not need to have a New Command to practice living by, He would not have given it to us, as a New Command to keep in our hearts to be compelled to live by.

The Holy Spirit of our GOD the Father and the Spirit of our Lord Jesus Christ is in every Child of GOD. Therefore, we must treat each other with the love of our Lord Jesus Christ to Always Love Each Other the way He showed us He loves us with His Life that He is so willing to give up for us to live eternal life. We must keep all the commandments of our Lord Jesus Christ because we are living in the appointed time of the New Covenant of the Spirit that gives Life. The Old Covenant has come to pass with our Lord Jesus Christ fulfilling all the prophecies in it, making it obsolete in glory by the surpassing glory of the New Covenant that He put into effect with His righteousness and the sacrifice of His Life for our sins that we repent. And now by His authority in the glory that was given to Him by our GOD the Father, by that authority He may bring the glory of eternal Life and rest it into all the believers in Him to be made Children of GOD.

We are not our own or left alone, we are made by THEM when we are re-formed with THEIR Spirits as One, in complete unity, to have them living within our Body-Temple with our personal Spirit forever. And like the Greatest of all commandments, Love GOD with all your Heart, Soul, and Mind, the New Command to Always Love Each Other is also so profound that we cannot live to enter eternal Life without living by it now.

The Greatest command is to Always Love our GOD the Father with our Soul, Heart, and Mind. The Second Greatest command is like the Greatest command, except the New Command is also for us to each other is for everyone to, Always Love Each Other including your neighbor. By that, we put the interest of all others before ourselves to show we love our Lord Jesus Christ and will be recognized as His disciples by learning and living by His Word of Truth.

We must do what the Word of Truth says and live by it, to have eternal Life, and to show our love for our Lord Jesus Christ, that we are His disciples. And just as our Lord Jesus Christ teaches us in the Word of Truth, we shall never think of putting anything above our loving GOD the Father. Only HE is good, and all goodness comes from HIS eternal Life power and through the Spirit of our Lord Jesus Christ, HIS Son who lives in us. Our Lord Jesus Christ always puts our GOD the Father above Himself and is always HIS Servant, because our GOD the Father is also the creator of our Lord Jesus Christ, creating Him as HIS first and only begotten Son before the Creation of the World. We must do the same as our Lord Jesus Christ and take the same humble mindset of Servant to our GOD the Father, and never, ever HIS equal as we live for HIM through His Son, our Lord Jesus Christ.

Our Lord Jesus Christ teaches us in the Word that there is only One GOD, and everyone is created by our GOD the Father, including our Lord Jesus Christ. As He said, He is the Son of GOD, and our GOD the Father is greater than our Lord Jesus Christ Himself; therefore, HE is greater than all. Our GOD the Father is looking for worshippers that worship HIM in Spirit giving thanks to HIM, through our Lord Jesus Christ, in the NAME of our Lord Jesus Christ, to honor HIS Son as we are taught to pray by our Lord Jesus Christ. When the ones that live and worship HIM in Spirit from within their Body-Temple now are redeemed on the Last Day, they will each be miraculously transformed spiritually into a New Spirit Body that is Holy and imperishable, to appear with our Lord Jesus Christ in the Holy presence of our GOD the Father.

If you are Baptized with the Holy Spirit, in the NAME of our Lord Jesus Christ, you must worship in Spirit to our GOD the Father, in the NAME of HIS Son Jesus Christ, in complete unity with THEM in you from now on. Do not fail to worship in Spirit because our GOD the Father looks for and hears those that worship HIM in Spirit and honor HIS Son, our Lord Jesus Christ by acknowledging Him by praying in His NAME JESUS. He is our Lord, He is our Savior, He is our Life within us. Our GOD the

Chapter 7: Jesus Christ our Friend...

Father is Spirit, HIS Holy Spirit is Spirit, our Lord Jesus Christ is Spirit, and we are also made with our personal Spirit living in our Body-Temple as One, formed with THEIR Spirits in complete unity.

Since you have our Lord Jesus Christ in you now with His Life giving you eternal Life, you have been forgiven and cleaned from any sin in you sanctified by our Lord Jesus Christ forgiving your sins and living in you. You have been reformed and made Holy by our Lord Jesus Christ and must continue to stay Holy with THEM, to keep the eternal Life which you have with THEM now, and forever after you are Raised up imperishable on the Last day, no matter where you are alive or dead in Christ Jesus.

Follow the guidance of the Holy Spirit of our GOD the Father living in you, as you live your life in your Spirit praising our GOD the Father in the NAME of HIS Son Jesus Christ forever. Our Lord Jesus Christ teaches us how to live Holy now by His commands and they are not burdensome. Knowing and keeping the commands of our Lord Jesus Christ is proving that you love Him. Be honest with yourself and don't be like a fool and say you keep His commands, and you don't take the time to know them first to put them into practice in your life now. Let's learn them together by praying in the Spirit every day to know them by heart.

Here are the commands of our Lord Jesus Christ:

1. (The Greatest command) Love GOD with all your Heart, Mind, and Soul.
2. Love your neighbor as yourself.
3. Do not murder.
4. Do not give false Testimony.
5. Do not steal.
6. Do not commit adultery.
7. Honor your mother and father.
8. (The New Command) Always Love Each Other. This is the Word, and it is the Truth.

- **Philippians 2:5-7 (NIV)**

    5 In your relationships with one another, have the same mindset as Christ Jesus: 6 Who, being in very nature GOD, did not consider equality with GOD, something to be used to His own advantage; 7 rather, He made Himself nothing by taking the very nature of a Servant, being made in Human Likeness.

All the Word, with all the commands in it, comes from and belongs to our GOD the Father, the creator of us all. But because people cannot see HIM with their own eyes, some will not believe HE exists. It is the same with HIS Holy Spirit. So, HE sent HIS first and only born, who is HIS one and only begotten Son, who was with our GOD the Father in Heaven before the Earth was created. Our GOD the Father sent Him in Spirit from Heaven to Earth and formed His Spirit with flesh in the womb of the blessed Woman Mary to birth Him. Then Human eyes would See Him, Hear Him, Touch Him, and Witness the miracles performed through Him, by the power of our Almighty GOD the Father dwelling in Him.

His Spirit lived in His Body-Temple until He committed His Own Spirit to our GOD the Father, before His death on the Cross, without sin. Then He was Raised Up by the Holy Spirit of our GOD the Father to return to our GOD the Father in Heaven. In the same way we will be raised up for having Him in our Body-Temple now at this appointed time, as we live with THEM in complete unity on Earth.

Our Lord Jesus Christ was with our GOD the Father before anything else was made and He deserves to be our Lord because He knows HIM the best and died for our sins with all His faith in our GOD the Father to restore Him to the Highest Grace at HIS Right-Hand side. So, now the World can believe what is written by the witnesses, to know our GOD

Chapter 7: Jesus Christ our Friend...

the Father is our Creator, and know that HE loves us so much HE gave us eternal Life through HIS Son. And by the CHOICE of HIS will for us, it is a gift for us to accept, by our own free will, by the Decision to live eternal Life in complete unity with THEM.

HE deserves our worship, because HE loves us and HE gave HIS only Son, our Lord Jesus Christ, the Word of Life, who willingly died without sin and shed His Blood as a Sin Offering, to forgive us of all our sins and give us eternal Life at the time we believe in Him, by believing and living by the Testimony of our GOD the Father, concerning HIS Son, with all our Heart, our Soul, and our Mind.

This is the Word, and it is the Truth.

- ### 1 John 5:10-12 (NIV)

    10 Whoever believes in the Son of GOD accepts this Testimony. Whoever does not believe GOD has made HIM out to be a liar, because they have not believed the Testimony GOD has given about HIS Son. 11 And this is the Testimony: **GOD has given us eternal Life, and this Life is in HIS Son. 12 Whoever has the Son has Life; Whoever does not have the Son of GOD does not have Life.**

- ### Matthew 19:17-19 (NIV)

    17 "Why do you ask Me about what is good?" Jesus replied. "There is only One GOD the Father who is good. If you want to enter Life, keep the commandments." 18...Jesus replied, You shall not Murder, you shall not Commit Adultery, you shall not Steal, you shall not Give False Testimony, 19 Honor your Father and Mother,' and 'Love your Neighbor as yourself.

The New Command is for us to, Always Love Each Other. Our Lord Jesus Christ also tells us; that He now calls us His friend. Because everything He learned from our GOD the Father is the Word and He has revealed it for us to know the Word and live by it. The first and greatest command is "Love GOD with all your Heart, Mind, and Soul". The New command is for us to Always Love Each Other means we must be friends as our Lord Jesus Christ is our friend who laid down His Life for us to give us Life through the death of His body that had no sin or ever sinned. The Word is now written in the New Testament of the Bible for our instruction with His New Command: "Always Love Each Other." We share the Word of Truth every day with each other because we have the love of our Lord Jesus Christ in our hearts that compels us to do what it says.

Stay connected to our Lord Jesus Christ and live in Him. He is our Church. Live by His commands in the Word and always keep it in your heart, your mind, and your soul for eternal Life. Your old life in the flesh of death, when you were "existing without" our Lord Jesus Christ in you, is done, dead, and over with. Now you are sanctified by learning, knowing, and living by the message in the Word and the commands in it. Remember, there is still an important commitment you will have to keep to stay committed if you haven't already done this. Knowing the message in the Word is enough for our sanctification but is not enough for our salvation.

Just as our Lord Jesus Christ did, you have to lay down your old life in the flesh of death and decide to submit and commit your Spirit to our GOD the Father, by praying in Spirit to HIM, in the NAME of our Lord Jesus Christ, to live in the Spirit with HIS Holy Spirit in complete unity. That is living with both the Holy Spirit of our GOD the Father and the Spirit of HIS Son, our Lord Jesus Christ, both living in you which is called living in complete unity with THEM. That is what our Lord prayed to our GOD the Father for us to have, to be One with THEM, as they are One with Each Other in Spirit. The Holy Spirit of our GOD the Father is how we are One with them. We have the same Holy Spirit that raised our

Chapter 7: Jesus Christ our Friend...

Lord Jesus Christ, living in us with our Spirit and will Raise us Up at our appointed time, to the glory of our GOD the Father in the NAME of HIS Son Jesus Christ our Lord.

Repentance alone is not receiving the Holy Spirit. Only those believing in our Lord Jesus Christ in their heart and doing what the Word says to do will be saved and receive the Holy Spirit. Believing in Him is doing what His Word says to do which includes each of us helping save others, by teaching them how to reconcile back to our GOD the Father. Teach others to keep all the Word and the commands in it, that are found in the Word and Gospel. You must remember to stay committed to our GOD the Father and to live by the Spirit the moment you believe the Testimony of our GOD the Father about HIS Son, our Lord Jesus Christ. And then learn to keep HIS commands by listening to what our Lord Jesus Christ is telling you through the Holy Spirit of our GOD the Father who guides you to the Truth at all times. Pay attention so He will keep you safe from evil and harm because THEY care about every little thing you do and know how important it is to communicate with you in thoughts and dreams while you are awake or asleep.

For those who want to be saved, you need to take the time that you need to submit and commit your Spirit in spiritual prayer to our GOD the Father and ask HIM to send you HIS Holy Spirit, in the NAME of our Lord Jesus Christ, to be living with THEM in complete unity with you. That is being Baptized with the Holy Spirit of our GOD the Father in the NAME of HIS Son Jesus Christ. You will have the Holy Spirit, but you will also have THEM all in complete unity within you. That is what our Lord Jesus Christ prayed for us, is to be in complete unity with THEM. Give all your praise and glory to our GOD the Father in the NAME of HIS Son, our Lord Jesus Christ.

At the moment that you believe without a doubt, you will receive the Holy Spirit to be living in your Body-Temple with your Spirit forever. Then pay attention to your Heart, Soul, and Mind, because the Holy Spirit is always guiding your Spirit from within your Body-Temple telling you what our Lord Jesus Christ wants you to say and do. And the Holy Spirit will guide your Spirit and Testify with your Spirit to our GOD the Father about everything you wish and need according to HIS Grand Plan for your life.

Living in the Spirit, with the Holy Spirit, is the Seal of HIS promise for eternal Life now, that you carry within you now, as a Holy Spirit Child of our GOD the Father. And HE will never leave you alone because HE knows HIS Holy Spirit is in you and you are HIS forever. HIS Holy Spirit will raise you up from wherever you are. Your Spirit will rise up to the Voice of our Lord Jesus Christ, for the redemption of the living in Spirit and complete unity on the Last Day. Knowing THEM is eternal Life for those who keep HIS commands and believe in the New Covenant of our GOD the Father.

Our Lord Jesus Christ said, "This is my command: Love Each Other as I have loved you."

- **Matthew 22 (NIV)**
  36 "Teacher, which is the greatest commandment in the Law?" 37 Jesus replied: "Love the LORD your GOD with all your Heart, and with all your Soul, and with all your Mind." 38 This is the First and Greatest Commandment. 39 And the Second is like it: "Love your neighbor as yourself." 40 all the Law and the prophets hang on these two commandments."

You must first keep the New Command to Always Love Each Other in order to feel compelled in your heart to keep all the other commandments. Then when it's your appointed time, and you have kept His commands, our Lord Jesus Christ may say to you, "I know you." And you may say to our Lord Jesus Christ, "My Lord Jesus Christ, I know You and our GOD the Father." You cannot enter eternal Life in the New Kingdom if you don't know our GOD the Father by HIS Holy

Chapter 7: Jesus Christ our Friend...

Spirit and have a spiritual relationship with the Spirit of our Lord Jesus Christ living in you right now, so that He may bring you to our GOD the Father from a Holy and Spiritual Life after your Body-Temple dies. You must have THEM within you living in your Body-Temple right now in complete unity to cross over from death to eternal Life and not be Judged.

This is our appointed time to show the World that we love THEM and believe the Testimony of our GOD the Father by our Decision to accept HIS New Covenant and live in the Spirit, by being guided by HIS Holy Spirit in complete unity with THEM now and forever. So, you have hope, HIS promise to HIS believers is eternal Life in the New World and in the New Kingdom with THEM. You will not see the shame by judgment at the appointed time reserved for the execution of the condemned wicked and condemned non-believers. That is who the Judgment Day and the final Second Death is reserved for. The true worshippers in the Spirit to our GOD the Father in the NAME of HIS Son Jesus Christ will not be part of that judgment because they have been made Holy to live Holy in Christ Jesus now and will be Raised Up Holy in our Lord Jesus Christ on that day.

- **Romans 10:9-11 (NIV)**

  9 If you Declare with your Mouth, "Jesus is Lord," and believe in your Heart that GOD raised Him from the dead, you will be saved. 10 For it is with your Heart that you believe and are justified, and it is with your Mouth that you profess your faith and are saved. 11 As scripture says, "Anyone who believes in Him will never be put to shame."

- **John 3:18 (NIV)**

  18 Whoever believes in Him is not condemned, but whoever does not believe stands condemned already, because they have not believed in the NAME of GOD'S One and only Son. ~ (Jesus Christ)

INSPIRATION FOR YOUR ETERNAL LIFE

- **John 5 (NIV)**
  <u>24</u> "***Very truly I tell you***, *Whoever hears My Word and believes HIM* (GOD the Father) *who sent Me* (Jesus Christ) *has eternal Life and will not be judged but has crossed over from death to Life.*

You must understand "how-to believe", so that you can cross over to eternal Life now, by having our Lord Jesus Christ in you now, so that you will not be judged. Without His helping you every step of your life now, you cannot cross over to eternal Life and live Holy and worship in Spirit now. Our GOD the Father is calling Humanity to a Holy Life to live now at this appointed time. So, you must find out now, and how, and what to do, and what not to do, to live by the commands in the written Word, to show you love THEM for helping you from certain doom by condemnation. And we do that by learning the message in the Word as a Disciple of our Lord Jesus Christ, and by keeping His commands. This is what we are doing, living and praying in Spirit right now.

Only our Lord Jesus Christ has the "authority to give" you eternal Life by removing your sin, so He may remain living in you, and Present you Holy, without any accusations or fault from sin to be Judged by when you appear with Him in the Presence of our GOD the Father. Now is our appointed time to prove that "we want to enter eternal Life", so we must get ready now, by living Holy now in Spirit. Our GOD the Father glorified HIS Son, our Lord Jesus Christ, with the Full power of Life in Him to give to whoever believes in Him. And HE appointed HIS Son Judge over all in Heaven, Earth, and Under Earth, to reconcile all things back to HIMSELF through HIS only begotten Son. By having our Lord Jesus Christ living in you now, you will live forever by the power of His eternal Life that is in Him living in you. You will not be judged on the Last Day, because you have already crossed over from death to eternal Life without sin in you. Your Spirit is now Holy with the Holy Spirit in

Chapter 7: Jesus Christ our Friend...

complete unity.

The Judgement Day is reserved for the wicked and non-believers, to be taken to their appointed place for their execution for being condemned by their Decision to stay condemned and to not believe in our GOD the Father and have HIS Son, our Lord Jesus Christ living in them as their Lord, which ultimately means they are calling GOD a liar by their actions and words.

- **John 5:22-24 (NIV)**
  22 Moreover, the Father judges no one, but has entrusted all judgment to the Son, 23 that all may honor the Son just as they honor the Father. Whoever does not honor the Son does not honor the Father, who sent Him. 24 **"Very truly I tell you***, Whoever hears My Word (Jesus Christ) and believes HIM (GOD the Father) who sent Me has eternal Life and will not be judged but has crossed over from death to Life.*

- **John 11:25-26 (NIV)**
  25 Jesus said to her, "I am the resurrection and the Life. The one who believes in Me will live, even though they die; (in Flesh) *26 and whoever lives* (now) *by believing in Me will never die.* (in Imperishable Spirit) *Do you believe this?"*

- **Colossians 1:19-22 (NIV)**
  19 For GOD was pleased to have all HIS fullness dwell in Him, 20 and through Him (Jesus Christ) *to reconcile to HIMSELF* (GOD the Father) *all things, whether things on Earth or things in Heaven, by making peace through His Blood shed on the cross. ~* (Jesus Christ) *21 Once you were alienated from GOD and were enemies in your minds because of your evil behavior. 22 But now HE has*

reconciled you by Christ's physical body through death to present you Holy in HIS sight, without blemish and free from accusation—.

—

Our lives depend on us having the Life of our Lord Jesus Christ living in us right now and forever. By the same NAME we ask of our GOD the Father, it's the same NAME our GOD the Father now protects us with. Have faith and bear fruit to show yourself to be disciples of our Lord Jesus Christ, and whatever you ask in the NAME of our Lord Jesus Christ to glorify our GOD the Father, HE will give to you through HIS Son who has been given that power of authority to give to you whatever our GOD the Father enables you to have.

This is the Word, and the Word is the Truth.

And This Is Our Prayer:

We pray to ask of You, our GOD the Father, to watch over us and our loved ones, as we keep the commands that You sent to us through Your Son, our Lord Jesus Christ, to teach us in Your Word. We pray to ask You in the NAME of Your Son, our Lord Jesus Christ.

Chapter 8: The World Hates the Disciples

John 15: 18-25 NIV

18 "If the World hates you, keep in mind that it hated Me first.

19 If you belonged to the World, it would love you as its own. As it is, you do not belong to the World, but I have chosen you out of the World. That is why the World hates you.

20 Remember what I told you: 'A servant is not greater than his Master.' If they persecuted Me, they will persecute you also. If they obeyed My Teaching, they will obey yours also.

21 They will treat you this way because of My NAME, for they do not know the ONE who sent Me.

22 If I had not come and spoken to them, they would not be guilty of sin; but now they have no excuse for their sin.

23 Whoever hates Me hates My Father as well.

24 If I had not done among them the works no one else did, they would not be guilty of sin. As it is, they have seen, and yet they have hated both Me and My Father.

25 But this is to fulfill what is written in their Law: 'They hated Me without reason.'

Chapter 8: The World Hates the Disciples

❖ Notice:

This is a warning to disciples that hate will come your way. When we speak with others, and share the Word that has sanctified our soul, we will be hated by some of them without reason. That hate without reason is a sin in itself. Do not hate them back. Stay humble, stand firm in faith, and keep the commands in the Word. Be cautious of them so that they don't corrupt you in their way of confusion. Do as our Lord Jesus Christ does and says to have the same mindset as He does about the people of the World. Remember what He said, about the ones that were killing Him, when He was crucified to die for our sins.

- Luke 23:34 (NIV)

    34 "Father, forgive them, for they do not know what they are doing."

Forgive, as our GOD the Father will forgive you for your sin and baptize you with HIS Holy Spirit to help you understand HIS righteousness with the same love HE has for our Lord Jesus Christ, HIS Son, love them and pray for them even as your enemies. And have patience with the love of our Lord Jesus Christ that what they see in you will make them want to turn from their sin and turn to Him for Life. They will remember that you never judged them, accused them, or shamed them, and only gave what you have in your heart to help them understand the love of our Lord Jesus Christ that comes from you. We can only teach, prove, and reprove the message in the Word to show others the righteous path that leads to eternal Life in our Lord Jesus Christ.

The miracle that changes us, comes through believing in our Lord Jesus Christ, and our GOD the Father. They make it happen for everyone who looks to our Lord Jesus Christ for the love and life in Him. He will not turn you or anyone away who believes in THEM and comes to Him for Life. His promise to you as His disciple is to raise you up to eternal Life with THEM. And your redemption is your reward with the Crown of eternal Life, Righteousness, and Glory for your faith by living in THEM. That will be yours on the Last Day when you are raised up Holy to be presented Holy as you had lived Holy on Earth from the time you accepted to believe in the Testimony of our GOD the Father. You will not be judged or shamed, just as our Lord Jesus Christ said in the Word. We all will see Him at His Throne in His glory to receive what we are promised for our decision to believe and accept Him as our Lord.

Only those who refuse to live with the Holy Spirit and the Spirit of our Lord Jesus Christ in themselves will be judged. Anyone who lived in complete unity with THEM in their Body- Temple will not be judged or put to shame by sin because they already live Holy now by glorifying our GOD the Father with HIS Holy Spirit through our Lord Jesus Christ in unity within themselves. They have already crossed over from death to eternal Life at this appointed time. Those who believed and lived by the Spirit will be transformed into imperishable Spirit Bodies and then receive the Crown of Righteousness in Heaven for their redemption to eternal Life in the New Kingdom with our GOD the Father, and HIS Son, our Lord Jesus Christ.

- ### Ezekiel 3:20-21 (NIV)

    20 "Again, when a righteous person turns from their righteousness and does evil, and I put a stumbling block before them, they will die. (GOD the Father) Since you did not warn them, they will die for their sin. The righteous things that person did will not be remembered, and I will hold you accountable for their blood. 21 But if you do warn the righteous person not to sin and they do not sin, they will surely live because they took warning, and you will have saved yourself.

Having the power of the Word in your heart inherently makes you responsible for helping others learn to keep the Word to save their Life;

Chapter 8: The World Hates the Disciples

and in turn saving your own life, by your good faith backed by your good deeds. That is bearing fruit that will last forever, and that is what pleases our GOD the Father. HIS Holy Spirit compels you from your heart as He tells you what to do and say to those who are being called to our Lord Jesus Christ for eternal Life. To please our GOD the Father you must always seek to be fruitful and to do the righteous things that will glorify HIM first. Good deeds with love toward the interest of others before our own interest is how we prove our worthiness and love for HIM.

Our eternal Life depends on our deeds in helping others with love, the same as our Lord Jesus Christ helped you reconcile to our GOD the Father with His love for you. We must carry forward everything that we know in the Word and Gospel of our Lord Jesus Christ as if we are saving ourselves and everyone that we love. Do that part and our Lord Jesus Christ will bless them without fail. Share the message in the Gospel about our GOD the Father and our Lord Jesus Christ to help others learn to know THEM and to have THEIR love living in themselves for eternal Life. Their eternal Life is depending on you to help them understand the Word. All the people you know and will know in your future are depending on you to share this Gospel with them by word or deed. Our deed is to get the Word to them and teach them how to accept the Spirit of our Lord Jesus Christ and the Holy Spirit into themselves.

Be bold and unashamed in your actions about yourselves believing in our Lord Jesus Christ, and others will see why you deserve His love and blessings with eternal Life. It's because you have the Spirit of Life from our Lord Jesus Christ alive in you, and it is by the power of His love and life that you will be inspired and compelled to express the love of our Lord Jesus Christ flowing through your heart and into everyone that hears you tell your Testimony to glorify Him and our GOD the Father. Because the love from the Holy Spirit is transcending love that comes out from your heart and into the heart of those that hear the Word through you, so they may understand and know the Word that is written in your heart.

The Holy Spirit writes the message in the Word of Truth into the hearts of everyone that believes in the Testimony of our GOD the Father and has HIS Son in them in complete unity to keep their inspiration for eternal Life strong. That is the Testimony of our GOD the Father. Others can feel the love you have for the Word written in your heart when they hear you speak about your Testimony of what it is to live in complete unity. That is your own inspiration for your eternal Life given to you to believe that our GOD the Father has Chosen for you to know HIM and HIS Son. And our Lord Jesus Christ will show Himself to you through the Holy Spirit to let you know that THEY are with you now and leading your life in righteousness and blessings, so that you will know without a doubt that they are with you for eternal Life. It is what we are given as a sign or a vision from our Lord Jesus Christ that makes us understand the Truth in the Word enough to then turn to our Lord Jesus Christ for Life.

Pray in Spirit giving thanks to glorify our GOD the Father, in the name of our Lord Jesus Christ, that those that appreciate your honesty and accept you to believe the Word as Truth can also accept to believe in our Lord Jesus Christ to have the love and life from Him in themselves. We must do whatever it takes in word or deed, as necessary, so they also may be anointed as you were by the will of our GOD the Father to have HIS love and life in themselves through our Lord Jesus Christ.

To have eternal life we must first accept to believe in the Testimony of our GOD the Father concerning our Lord Jesus Christ. Then we are expected to share the Word of Truth with others to Testify to them about the love and the eternal Life in ourselves that we experience every day. And by the love that we experience with our Lord Jesus Christ to help us overcome our own old habits of sinful nature, we can teach others how to remain clean and Holy in our Lord Jesus Christ since we have already crossed over from death to eternal Life with Him helping us.

We already learned and know the Way, the Life, and the Truth is through having our Lord Jesus Christ in complete unity, now we must show others the Way, the Life, and the Truth in Him to do the same for themselves with the love of our Lord Jesus Christ. We can only do that because we have the Spirit of our Lord Jesus Christ and the Holy Spirit helping us

Chapter 8: The World Hates the Disciples

from within us. We are living in the time where we are called to help sow the Word of Truth into the hearts of believers until our Lord Jesus Christ reaps them from the Earth to raise them up with all the ones we love to our home with Him in the New Kingdom. Let the power of our GOD the Father with the help of our Lord Jesus Christ flow through you and into others as HE commands us to do, to bring everyone HE is calling to HIM for eternal Life.

- **1 John 5:10-12 (NIV)**
  10 Whoever believes in the Son of GOD accepts this Testimony. Whoever does not believe GOD has made HIM out to be a liar, because they have not believed the Testimony GOD has given about HIS Son. 11 And this is the Testimony: **GOD has given us eternal Life, and this Life is in HIS Son.** *12* **Whoever has the Son has Life; Whoever does not have the Son of GOD does not have Life.**

Everyone who believes this Testimony of our GOD the Father and is living by it every day and know without a doubt that they already have eternal Life now. And anyone that doesn't believe the Truth in the Word is a liar and stands condemned for not believing in the NAME of our Lord Jesus Christ and the Testimony of our GOD the Father.

Be patient, sometimes it takes more time for some to turn to our Lord Jesus Christ to be forgiven for their sin and accept to have Him within themselves for eternal Life. It may be because they don't yet believe they can be forgiven for the sin they committed. Or they may be judging themselves for their own acts in condemnation and have too much self-righteous pride in themselves to repent. Or they are just ashamed to bring up the past for their lack of courage, due to their own lack of faith for not knowing the Word of Truth from our GOD the Father. Like everyone else who has been saved, we all must take the leap of faith and trust in the Word of Truth that this miracle will happen to them as long as they make the effort to go to our Lord Jesus Christ to be forgiven for their sins and then strive to follow the righteous path of life with THEM in complete unity.

We must show them how to pray in Spirit to our GOD the Father in the NAME of our Lord Jesus Christ. Tell them the Word of Truth in the power of calling on the NAME of our Lord Jesus Christ and how He has answered your prayer to help you in your life, which is telling your Testimony of how the Holy Spirit has guided you throughout your life, especially how you know without a doubt that He is living and working through you every moment of your Life.

Our GOD the Father is not asking you to make or do something you can't make or do, because HE knows you can't make or do anything without HIM. He made the choice for you and established the steps for you to answer HIS calling you, to bring you to HIMSELF through believing in the NAME of HIS Son, our Lord Jesus Christ. That is the New Covenant and HIS Testimony. That is HIS promise to the World that includes you, your children, and everyone that you love and care for, and it is to give you all eternal life if you believe in HIM without a doubt that HE sent HIS Son for our salvation and live by HIS commands. To show that you love the Son our Lord Jesus Christ you must keep His commands that He teaches us to Always Love Each Other the way He loves us. This is His message to us for each other.

If you have it in your heart to believe and accept HIS Testimony, that is HIS New Covenant of the Spirit, you only need to Decide by your own free will to accept HIS Choice for yourself to have eternal Life with THEM. If you repent your sin with all your Heart, Mind, and Soul, your fear and shame will be forgiven by our Lord Jesus Christ. And you will be set free from that burden forever. There is no need for you to live in fear any longer than you have because the New Covenant of the Spirit is your first step toward eternal Life starting at the moment you believe in the Testimony of our GOD the Father and accept HIS Son, who is our Lord Jesus Christ, into your Body-Temple for eternal Life now and for

Chapter 8: The World Hates the Disciples

redemption after your Body- Temple dies. Your Spirit will be remembered and raised up by the Holy Spirit at the sound of the Voice from our Lord Jesus Christ calling you up to Himself in the Heavens with the rest of your family who have accepted our Lord Jesus Christ into their heart.

Judging ourselves is the way Satan wants us to stay thinking, so we don't turn from sin and go to our Lord Jesus Christ with our sins to be forgiven and to be given eternal Life. He lost the right to eternal Life when he lost his place in Heaven for his lies and transgressions against our GOD the Father. Satan wants us to stand condemned and be accused of sin to be judged for our Spirit to be put to death in the Second Death for living in condemnation on the Last Day, the Judgement Day for the condemned. He wants to keep us from living with our GOD the Father as our GOD the Father originally intended us to be living with HIM for eternal Life when HE first created Humanity in Paradise.

All those that continue to stay living condemned already on the Last Day will be raised to the Throne of Judgement and be put to death of their Spirit for not accepting to have our Lord Jesus Christ with them and by not accepting doing the will of our GOD the Father in their body before the Judgement Day. This is the appointed time in our lives for us to prove that we want to accept the love our GOD the Father by doing HIS will because we love HIM and HIS Son. This is exactly what our Lord Jesus Christ teaches us in the Word of Truth.

This is the Word of our GOD the Father, and it is the Word of Truth.

We must bring our shame from sin, that we are ashamed of, to our Lord Jesus Christ and into the light to prove that we repent for what we have done and regret it. All Humanity already stands condemned and doomed to destruction because of sin that separates us from the Holy presence of our GOD the Father. But the ones that find the Truth in the Word to believe the Gospel and do what it says to do can begin to live with the eternal Life that is in our Lord Jesus Christ. He already knows our sin; you cannot hide it from Him and His will is to forgive us now. It is up to us to accept His gift that He has already fulfilled in the New Covenant and given His Life for us. All you have to do is believe in Him, that He was sent by our GOD the Father, and turn to Him to be forgiven forever for the sin you repent. And the power of His love and the Life in Him will make you a Holy Child of our GOD the Father with the right to live a Holy Life in Spirit and in complete unity with THEM now and later in the Kingdom of Heaven forever.

———

Your forgiveness for others and yourself is between you and our Lord Jesus Christ, the only One given the Authority to give Life to others by the will of our GOD the Father to forgive you of your sin and give you eternal Life now. Keep what you have sinned to yourself, so no one can falsely accuse you of having sin in you after you have been forgiven. Because no one else has the authority to condemn your Spirit, save your Spirit, or forgive anyone's sin, except our Lord Jesus Christ, who was glorified by our GOD the Father and HE has given Him the power of eternal Life in Himself with All Authority over all in Heaven, Earth, and Under Earth, to reconcile all things to HIMSELF through our Lord Jesus Christ.

Therefore, no one else on Earth ever needs to hear what you have repented for in your prayer in Spirit to our GOD the Father through our Lord Jesus Christ for your salvation. Pray in Spirit and repent your sin in privacy only to our GOD the Father in the NAME of HIS Son, Jesus Christ the only One that will legitimately forgive you and make you clean, Holy, and without sin. That business is between each person and our Lord Jesus Christ our Savior, who is the only One that has the authority to forgive sin and give eternal Life to whomever believes in Him.

Bend no knee before anyone or anything except for our Lord Jesus Christ and our GOD the Father, who both love you and have the will with the power to restore you from any hardship and the condemnation from this World of corruption. And the will of our Lord Jesus Christ is the will

Chapter 8: The World Hates the Disciples

of our GOD the Father, which is to care for you for eternal Life. Only our GOD the Father deserves our Worship through HIS Son, our Lord Jesus Christ. But more importantly, we must first learn to believe in our Lord Jesus Christ and His great power of Life that our GOD the Father has put in Him to forgive us now on Earth. Bring all your sins to our Lord Jesus Christ and truly repent for all your sins, because His will is to wash your sins away, and tell you, you are forgiven. And then He will raise you up to eternal Life with THEM, to fulfill the command that is the will of our GOD the Father. He is the only way for you to "cross over from death to eternal Life". You must have Him in Spirit, in complete unity, in your Body-Temple. At that time you also cross over from living for flesh to death, to living for Spirit with eternal Life.

The New Covenant is for us to believe in and know our GOD the Father and have our Lord Jesus Christ living within us for eternal Life in Spirit. All those that have Him and the Holy Spirit of our GOD the Father living within them in complete unity are living their eternal Life now, with their personal Spirit within their Body-Temple. By being forgiven now and living with the Spirit of our Lord Jesus Christ and the Holy Spirit in complete unity with you now, guarantees that you will not need to be judged on the Judgement Day any more than our Lord Jesus Christ because He already removed your sin and made you Holy as One with THEM. You are living a Holy Life to be presented Holy with the Holy Spirit of our GOD the Father and with the Spirit of our Lord Jesus Christ as One.

You will not see shame or judgment if you have the Spirit of our Lord Jesus Christ now. Truly believing in our Lord Jesus Christ, and that He was sent from Heaven by our GOD the Father to shed His Blood and die as an innocent Man for us as a Sin Offering of Himself once and for all, to fulfill the only sacrifice that could free us of our sin for our salvation from death, is believing in the power of the New Covenant of the Spirit that gives Life and was made for us by the mercy of our GOD the Father who loves us.

In this appointed time on Earth, you will become whoever or whatever you believe in and follow in that way. If you believe in nothing you will be nothing, since you are already condemned without eternal Life now anyway. Or if you believe in an inanimate object that has no power to give life, you will not have life because you are already condemned anyway. If you believe in Satan and follow him or anyone that is like Satan that is condemned, you are condemned already because of evil anyway. If you believe in anything or anyone in any way that cannot give you eternal Life you stand condemned anyway. Saying you believe in a higher power, and you don't know or care to find out who or what it is, or what the higher power expects of you, or if that higher power really exists, then you stand condemned anyway.

Living without having our Lord Jesus Christ in you, is living in vain and condemnation already from the sin of not believing in the Testimony of our GOD the Father, which is calling HIM a liar, to your doom and destruction of your personal Spirit in the Second Death. That goes for all non-believers in our Lord Jesus Christ as He taught in the Word of Truth. According to the Testimony of our GOD the Father, only by believing in and accepting our Lord Jesus Christ is the only way for us to be forgiven for our sins and to live a Holy Life in Spirit, to have eternal life without sin right now.

This is the Word, and it is the Truth.

Forgive others for the pain they caused you by their hate towards you and give it all to our Lord Jesus Christ by prayer in Spirit. Our Lord Jesus Christ explains, that He would be hated and was hated first because they did not know our GOD the Father. So, they could not possibly know the mercy HE has for us, or how HE thinks, speaks, and acts. They did not understand our GOD the Father was showing HIS love for us through our Lord Jesus Christ by sacrificing the flesh and Sacred Blood of HIS Son, in His innocence, for the sin in our flesh and our sinful blood to be forgiven and made into Sacred Blood in all those who believe in Him.

They did not believe it was possible, that HIS Word was being spoken through HIS Son, our Lord Jesus Christ. They did not know that the

Chapter 8: The World Hates the Disciples

power of the miracles that our Lord Jesus Christ performed, came through Him from the power of our GOD the Father dwelling in Him. And they did not believe our Lord Jesus Christ when He told them who, what, why, and how everything He said and did, was our GOD the Father doing HIS own works through our Lord Jesus Christ to reconcile Mankind back to HIMSELF. That is exactly what HE promised to our ancient ancestors HE would do as it is written in the Old Testament of the Bible, the Old Covenant that has been fulfilled by our Lord Jesus Christ in the New Covenant of the Spirit that gives eternal Life and glory to our GOD the Father in Heaven who brings eternal Life to us.

"Not believing the Truth in the Word of our GOD the Father is a sin", as our Lord Jesus Christ teaches by the Truth in the Word. And that is the sin that the wicked and the non-believers commit by their ignorance and hate of the Word of GOD the Father. It's as bad as calling our GOD the Father and also our Lord Jesus Christ a liar. To think anything our Lord Jesus Christ said is not true is a lie.

Therefore, reproach the thoughts of non-believers, or any lie that may cross your mind, and strike it from your mind in the NAME of our Lord Jesus Christ. Remember, the minds of believers in our Lord Jesus Christ belong to our GOD the Father. Protect your Heart, Mind, and Soul with the Word of Truth for eternal Life. Hating without reason is the same as "Bearing False Testimony" against our Lord Jesus Christ. That is not obeying His command, that we are not to Bear False Testimony by anything we say or do.

By not proclaiming that you believe in the Testimony of our GOD the Father is calling HIM a liar by your actions of not acknowledging what HE and our Lord Jesus Christ have done for us to have the gift of eternal Life. He certainly is not a liar, and He only speaks the Word of Truth. Our Lord Jesus Christ never committed a sin, and He keeps all the commands of our GOD the Father in Heaven which shows He loves HIM. If we all keep the New Command to "Always Love Each Other", our common sense will keep all other commands including the Greatest commands.

- **Mathew 22:37-39 (NIV)**
  37 Jesus replied: "'Love the LORD your GOD with all your heart and with all your Soul and with all your Mind.' 38 This is the First and Greatest Commandment. 39 And the second is like it: 'Love your neighbor as yourself.'

Remember, GOD the Father is glorified and pleased by us, because we bear fruit by sharing HIS Word of Truth to help sanctify the souls of anyone who seeks HIM and HIS Word and believes in THEM. We will hear rejection, but that rejection is not entirely for you, it's also for the One who sent you out with the Word, our Lord Jesus Christ, that lives in you now. Do not be afraid of hate, that hate is a sin. We have overcome all hate and all sin as we know it by the Spirit of our Lord Jesus Christ living in us. Remember, that hate in non-believers is only their weakness in themselves for not being willing to understand the Truth in the Word. Hate is the ignorance of not knowing and believing the Truth in the Word provided by our GOD the Father through HIS Son our Lord Jesus Christ.

All those who accept to live by the Word and believe the Testimony of our GOD the Father concerning our Lord Jesus Christ will be saved. Our GOD the Father and HIS Son, our Lord Jesus Christ, will come to us and make THEIR home with us. They will dwell with us forever in a New Heaven that will be conjoined with a New Earth that our GOD the Father will create for us to live in with HIM and without any suffering.

- **Revelations 21 (NIV)**
  1 Then I saw a New Heaven and a New Earth, for the First Heaven and the First Earth had passed away, and there was no longer any sea. 2 I saw the Holy City, the New Jerusalem, coming down out of Heaven from GOD,

Chapter 8: The World Hates the Disciples

prepared as a bride beautifully dressed for her husband. 3 And I heard a Loud Voice from the Throne saying, "Look! GOD'S Dwelling Place is now among the people, and HE will dwell with them. They will be HIS People, and GOD HIMSELF will be with them and be their GOD. 4 'HE will wipe every tear from their eyes. There will be no more death or mourning or crying or pain, for the Old Order of things has passed away." 5 HE who was seated on the Throne said, "I am making everything new!"

AND THIS IS OUR PRAYER:

We ask You in prayer, our GOD the Father, to make us fearless and bold to speak Your Holy Word of Truth to others with the love You send through us. Make us more fruitful as we help others learn to keep Your Word of Truth, so they may also glorify You and Your Son, our Lord Jesus Christ. We love You, our GOD the Father, with all our heart, our Soul, and our Mind.

We ask of You in the NAME of Your only begotten Son, our Lord Jesus Christ.

Chapter 9: Holy Spirit will Testify…You also must

John 15: 26-27 NIV

<u>26</u> "When the Advocate comes, whom I will send to you from the Father—The Spirit of Truth who goes out from the Father—(Holy Spirit) He will Testify about Me. (Jesus Christ)

<u>27</u> And you also must Testify, for you have been with Me from the beginning.

❖ **Notice:**

Our Lord Jesus Christ tells us the source of the Holy Spirit is from our GOD the Father. The Holy Spirit is also referred to as; The Spirit, He, His, Him, Holy Ghost, HIS Spirit, Helper, Advocate, Counselor, Spirit of Truth, Spirit of GOD.

We are given eternal Life to be saved from certain death by the mercy and love of our GOD the Father giving eternal Life to us through the power of the Spirit of Life that HE put in our Lord Jesus Christ when our GOD the Father glorified HIS Son again in Heaven at His return to our GOD the Father in Heaven. The only way to be saved is to have the Life of our Lord Jesus Christ living in us by first believing in the Testimony of our GOD the Father and giving thanks to HIM for HIS mercy on us. Then ask our GOD the Father to send us HIS Holy Spirit in the NAME of our Lord Jesus Christ, while praying in Spirit through our Lord Jesus

Chapter 9: Holy Spirit will Testify...You Also Must

Christ to forgive us for the sin that we repent; which is also acknowledging that we believe the power in NAME of our Lord Jesus Christ that we call on to fulfill us to the Righteous Requirement to be Holy in the sight of our GOD the Father, and that we accept the Spirit of our Lord Jesus Christ that our GOD the FATHER sends to us to be in us as our Savior for eternal Life.

That means we become spiritually united with our Lord Jesus Christ who is One in Spirit with our GOD the Father; therefore, our personal Spirit is One in Spirit with both the Spirit of our Lord Jesus Christ and with the Holy Spirit of our GOD the Father, all within our Body-Temple in complete unity. Therefore, we are made spiritually reformed with THEIR Spirits becoming One with our personal Spirit. And the power of inspiration from THEM within your reformed Spirit will allow you see, do, and say whatever you need to be saved from evil. You will always have both in complete unity within your Body-Temple helping you remember the Word of Truth that you learned to guide you throughout your life now and forever. The Spirit of Life is in our Lord Jesus Christ, and the Spirit of Life lives together with your personal Spirit in your Body-Temple and gives you eternal Life. And of course, you will not have sin in you anymore because your sins are legitimately forgiven at the first time you begin to believe in Him, and just before the Spirit of our Lord Jesus Christ will start to live in you with the Holy Spirit of our GOD the Father guiding your personal Spirit, all within your Body-Temple. You have been given more grace than you had by the love and mercy of our GOD the Father who will be with you forever.

When you are saved from condemnation, you have our Lord Jesus Christ and eternal Life with the Life that was put in Him by our GOD the Father, and now His Life is your Life. Therefore, the Testimony of our GOD the Father is:

- **1 John 5:11-12 (NIV)**
  11 And this is the Testimony: **GOD has given us eternal**

> ***Life, and this Life is in HIS Son.** 12 **Whoever has the Son has Life; whoever does not have the Son of GOD does not have Life**.*

———

"Whoever has the Son has eternal Life." - That is having the Spirit of His eternal Life that is in our Lord Jesus Christ, to be living in you. Keep in mind, you also have the Seal of our GOD the Father in you, the Holy Spirit that comes out from HIM and into you, in the NAME of our Lord Jesus Christ. That is the Holy Spirit, who tells us what our Lord Jesus Christ wants us to know and guides your personal Spirit from within you forever. That is why our Lord Jesus Christ said, "… but, you know Him". (Holy Spirit) Because He is living with you and will be in you forever.

They will be in us, in complete unity, at this appointed time giving life to our Mortal Bodies. believers are One with them now and forever by the will of our GOD the Father, who has given us eternal Life with His New Covenant of the Spirit that gives us eternal Life, which was completely fulfilled by the will of HIS Son, our Lord Jesus Christ. The gift of eternal Life has already been prepared and given in our Lord Jesus Christ for anyone who goes to Him for Life. We must turn to our Lord Jesus Christ to have Life. And whomever believes in the Testimony of our GOD the Father and Decide to accept living by it, is accepting HIS New Covenant of the Spirit and to live in complete unity with THEM now and forever. That makes you Holy in your Body-Temple now.

It is our responsibility to continue to believe in THEM and stay Holy, or we will be cut off by our GOD the Father, as our Lord Jesus Christ teaches us in the Word about the Gardener, the Vine, and the Branch. Be fruitful and our GOD the Father will love you more than you can imagine. He will help you become stronger in faith and deed to bring you into the New Kingdom to live forever. This is eternal Life for you and your family now, by having our Lord Jesus Christ in you. Our Lord Jesus Christ knows that you love your children, and He will be with them as your heart desires, because you will have prayed in Spirit for their protection, in the NAME of our Lord Jesus Christ to glorify our GOD the Father. Teach everyone that you love the Testimony of our GOD the Father to glorify Him.

- ## John 14:16-17 (NIV)
  16 And I will ask the Father, and HE will give you another Advocate to help you and be with you forever— 17 The Spirit of Truth. The World cannot accept Him, because it neither sees Him nor knows Him. But you know Him, for He lives with you and will be in you.

- ## Romans 8 N.I.V.,
  1 Therefore, there is now no condemnation for those who are living in Christ Jesus, 2 because through Christ Jesus the Law of the Spirit (New Covenant) *who gives Life has set you free from the law of sin and death.* (Old Covenant) *3 For what the law* (Old Covenant) *was powerless to do because it was weakened by the flesh,* **GOD did by sending HIS own Son**, *in the likeness of sinful flesh, to be a Sin Offering. And so, He condemned sin in the flesh, 4 in order that the Righteous Requirement of the Law might be fully met in us, who do not live according to the flesh, but* (live) *according to the Spirit.* (New Covenant) *5 Those who live according to the flesh have their minds set on what the flesh desires* (in the World); *but those who live in accordance with the Spirit have their minds set on what the Spirit desires* (in Heaven). *6 The mind governed by the flesh is death,* (Old Covenant) *but the mind governed by the Spirit is Life and Peace.* (New Covenant) *7 The mind governed by the flesh is hostile to GOD; it does not submit to GOD'S Law, nor can it do so. 8 Those who are in the realm of the flesh cannot please GOD. 9 You, however, are not in the Realm of the flesh but are in the Realm of the Spirit, if indeed the Spirit of GOD lives in you. And if anyone does not have the*

Spirit of Christ, they do not belong to Christ. 10 But if Christ is in you, then even though your body is subject to death because of sin, the Spirit gives Life because of righteousness. 11 And if the Spirit of HIM (Holy Spirit of GOD the Father) *who raised Jesus from the dead is living in you, He* (Holy Spirit of GOD the Father) *who raised Christ from the dead will also give Life to your Mortal Bodies* (now) *because of HIS Spirit* (Holy Spirit) *who lives in you. 12 Therefore, Brothers and Sisters, we have an obligation—but it is not to the flesh, to live according to it. 13 For if you live according to the flesh, you will die; but if* (living) *by the Spirit* (personal Spirit) *you put to death the misdeeds of the body, you will live. 14 For those who are led by the Spirit of GOD are the Children of GOD. 15 The Spirit you received does not make you slaves, so that you live in fear again; rather, the Spirit you received brought about your Adoption to Sonship. And by Him* (Holy Spirit) *we cry, "ABBA, Father." 16 The Spirit Himself Testifies with our Spirit that we are GOD'S Children.*

The Holy Spirit compels our personal Spirit to call out to our GOD the Father in our spiritual prayer, and that is how the Holy Spirit Testifies with our Spirit that we are the Children of the One and only GOD the Father that we worship and call to in Spirit prayer, in the NAME of HIS Son, our Lord Jesus Christ. We are living in complete unity with THEM by the Word. So, it shall be done, in the NAME of Jesus, our Lord, and Savior for eternal Life.

This is the Word, and it is the Truth.

Now you have all this power and support working with you, to help others reconcile back to our GOD the Father for eternal Life. As a Disciple of our Lord Jesus Christ and living in the Spirit by the Word of Truth, you have a fellowship between your personal Spirit, that you were born within your Body-Temple, and the Holy Spirit from our GOD the Father living in you now.

Chapter 9: Holy Spirit will Testify...You Also Must

The "baptism in water" was what John the Baptist did for the repenting of sin for the people at that time. That is not the baptism that gives anyone the Holy Spirit, he did not have that authority. And we are not saved by our repentance alone, but with the power of Life that was set into our Lord Jesus Christ by our GOD the Father in Heaven. Our Lord Jesus Christ, who sits at the Right Hand of our GOD the Father, has been given the Authority to give eternal life to whomever He desires by the will of our GOD the Father. We must accept them both in us to help us live a Holy Life in complete unity. Without the Spirit of our Lord Jesus Christ living in us, we are nothing and can do nothing without accepting Him within ourselves.

- ### Acts 19:3-6 (NIV)
    3 So Paul asked, "Then what baptism did you receive?" "John's baptism," they replied. 4 Paul said, "John's baptism was a baptism of repentance. He told the people to believe in the One coming after him, that is, in Jesus." 5 On hearing this, they were baptized in the NAME of the Lord Jesus. 6 When Paul placed his hands on them, the Holy Spirit came on them, and they spoke in tongues and prophesied.

Do not expect to speak in tongues, a "foreign language" when you are anointed by receiving the Holy Spirit. Not everyone will be enabled to speak in tongues when they are baptized in the NAME of our Lord Jesus Christ. It is the Holy Spirit that "enables" a person with the gift of speaking in tongues as He sees fit and when He sees that it is necessary to bring someone who speaks a foreign language to learn the message in the Word to become a believer and accept our Lord Jesus Christ as their Lord and Savior. If you are enabled to speak in tongues, good, get to work because it is your responsibility to find others who know that language and prophesy to those people, to be fruitful and help them understand the Gospel in their native language.

There are many other things that you can be blessed with by the Holy Spirit at any time necessary to help others get saved from condemnation. Those who do speak in "other languages" must speak with an interpreter listening and translating to allow all disciples to understand what they are saying in a church gathering to help those who do not understand your foreign language to learn the Word of Truth. Otherwise, they must not speak in other tongues and remain quiet so others can learn the Gospel and the Word of Truth in their own language intelligently. Remember, you are responsible for every word that comes out of your mouth, even idle words.

- ### 1 Corinthians 14:27-28 (NIV)
  27 If anyone speaks in a tongue, two- or at the most three- should speak, one at a time, and someone must interpret. 28 If there is no interpreter, the speaker should keep quiet in the church and speak to himself and to GOD.

Therefore, you may have the Holy Spirit and not be enabled to speak in tongues. Only by knowing our GOD the Father and HIS Son, our Lord Jesus Christ, can we have eternal Life and have the Holy Spirit within us enabling us with whatever miraculous gifts necessary to help us bring others to reconcile with our GOD the Father.

This is the Word, and it is the Truth.

Believers need to know; that the baptism of our Lord Jesus Christ is being filled with the Holy Spirit of our GOD the Father and the Spirit of our Lord Jesus Christ in themselves. And that is carried out at once, at the time you first believe in our Lord Jesus Christ, by believing that our GOD the Father sent Him to us to give us eternal Life. Then you must live by His commands now, to remain Holy now, in complete unity. Believing is you accepting Him to do His will, which is also living by all His commands you have learned in the Written Word.

Chapter 9: Holy Spirit will Testify...You Also Must

Being filled with the Holy Spirit and Fire is our Body-Temple being baptized and filled with the Holy Spirit into our Body-Temple. The Holy Spirit is sent in the NAME of our Lord Jesus Christ who has the Authority over all creation to give eternal Life. Exactly what John the Baptist said that our Lord Jesus Christ would do for us is happening and is happening in this appointed time, to make us Holy Children now before the Lord's Day comes. That is the Last Day when He calls us up with a Loud Voice and we are raised up to be instantly transformed into imperishable Spirit Bodies in the Heavens. Because no one else, then or now, has been given that Authority to send and Baptize with the Holy Spirit and Fire; except through our Lord Jesus Christ. And those that are Holy Children of our GOD the Father now can help and ask through our Lord Jesus Christ, in the NAME of Jesus Christ, while giving thanks to our GOD the Father in Spirit prayer, to send HIS Holy Spirit into those that have repented their sins to our Lord Jesus Christ.

If a person has the ability to learn the written Word of Truth enough to believe it and become sanctified, then they may repent their sins by praying in Spirit in the NAME of our Lord Jesus Christ while giving thanks to our GOD the Father and ask of HIM to send HIS Holy Spirit into themselves to submit and commit themselves to glorify our GOD the Father and it shall be done without delay. That is the promise of our Lord Jesus Christ. To either one you ask, the Father or the Son, to send the Holy Spirit in the NAME of our Lord Jesus Christ while giving thanks to glorify our GOD the Father, it shall be done without delay and the Holy Spirit of our GOD the Father will be within you forever. Because our Lord Jesus Christ has been given the Authority to send the Holy Spirit of our GOD the Father to anyone who turns from their sin and goes to Him for eternal Life.

That is why our Lord Jesus Christ teaches us how we must pray in Spirit to our GOD the Father and ask on our own behalf for anything we need to glorify our GOD the Father. You must have the courage and will to at least do that on your own behalf for yourself. Our Lord Jesus Christ will not do that for you, you must submit and commit yourself to our GOD the Father because you know He loves you and that it is His will and Choice to give you eternal Life already. It is up to you to accept it by your own Decision, by asking on your own behalf to accept His Choice for you. You are then made Holy and must remain Holy by living by the commands in the Word because you have crossed over from death to Life, from being condemned to not being condemned, by having salvation with eternal Life with the Holy Spirit of our GOD the Father and the Spirit of our Lord Jesus Christ helping you in complete unity.

Our Lord Jesus Christ has been given the Authority of Life in Him by our GOD the Father, to give eternal life to whoever believes in Him at any time anyone believes in Him without doubt. That is the miracle within you, when our GOD the Father sets His Holy Spirit in you, to give Life to your Mortal Body "now", for you to have eternal Life "now", until His promise in you is redeemed on the Last Day for you to have eternal Life in the New Kingdom, with a new imperishable Spirit Body that you will be transformed into, instantly, when you hear the Voice of our Lord Jesus Christ calling you to raise you up to Himself in Heaven. Our Lord Jesus Christ has been given the Authority to baptize with the Holy Spirit and Fire, and by the Holy Spirit of our GOD the Father, you will be raised up to be completely restored.

That is why, after He died and returned to our GOD the Father in Heaven, our Lord Jesus Christ did ask our GOD the Father to send us His Holy Spirit to live in us now. So, we may live a Holy Life now to give glory to our GOD the Father, and HIS Son, our Lord Jesus Christ. We are called to a Holy Life to live eternal in complete unity with THEM.

- **2 Timothy 1:9 (NIV)**

    9 He has saved us and called us to a Holy Life—Not because of anything we have done, but because of HIS own purpose and grace. This grace was given to us in Christ Jesus before the beginning of Time.

Chapter 9: Holy Spirit will Testify...You Also Must

Unless He returned and asked, the Holy Spirit that goes out of our GOD the Father would not have come to rest in us. The Holy Spirit of our GOD the Father and your Spirit will Testify together as One because His Holy Spirit is living in you. And that is your Spirit relationship with the Holy Spirit living in you.

The Holy Spirit enabled some of the disciples the gift of speaking in tongues to speak to other Nationalities in their Native Language at that time, to prophesy the Gospel and teach them the commands in the Word of Truth that our Lord Jesus Christ taught to the Apostles. Their language in foreign tongues was clearly understood by many thousands of people for days, to baptize them in the NAME of Jesus Christ for them to receive the Holy Spirit. The only purpose for the gift of speaking in tongues is to be fruitful with it; to bring others to glorify our GOD the Father in their Native Language. Miraculously speaking in other tongues is never meant to be a display of babbling without knowing what you are saying. You are held accountable for every word you speak out of your mouth, even your idle words. And no matter what language you are enabled to speak, you will know exactly what to say because our Lord Jesus Christ will tell you what to say and do by the Holy Spirit in you. What we read in the scripture was a time of Holy baptism with the Holy Spirit filling believers with knowledge to communicate with every Nationality of people from the Region, in their (tongue) language to reconcile them all to our GOD the Father HIMSELF.

In the Old Testament, Our GOD the Father appeared to Moses in a "Pillar of Fire," to show where HIS Temple was to be built, and where HIS Holy Spirit will rest with the people. And in the New Testament, after the resurrection of our Lord Jesus Christ, now it is within each of our Body-Temple of the saved where the Holy Spirit of our GOD the Father will now rest upon with our personal Spirit. And the Holy Spirit will be living with our personal Spirit forever.

We are each like one building block of a Temple, and our Lord Jesus Christ is the Cornerstone of that Temple, made true and perfect on all sides. As we are all lined up with Him and lean on His perfection, we are attached to Him, and become one with Him in unity. We are given a true and straight setting on every side of us, in our place as being part of the Temple that belongs to the Creator that plans, forms, and establishes all creation, who formed each of us from our personal Spirit in Heaven and with our flesh on Earth, HE is our GOD the Father. Together we are spiritually united in our Lord Jesus Christ, and the power of the Holy Spirit of our GOD the Father dwells in Him. We are in complete unity with THEM now.

- Romans 8:16-17 N.I.V.,
  16 The Spirit Himself Testifies with our Spirit that we are GOD's Children. 17 Now if we are Children, then we are Heirs—Heirs of GOD and Co-Heirs with Christ, if indeed we share in His sufferings in order that we may also share in His glory.

Our Lord Jesus Christ returned to Heaven and asked our GOD the Father to send His Holy Spirit to His Apostles and all disciples in the NAME of HIS Son, Jesus Christ. And, as we are baptized as disciples of our Lord Jesus Christ now; out from our GOD the Father, in the NAME of our Lord Jesus Christ, the Holy Spirit comes directly into our Body-Temple, and rests in us. Our GOD the Father knows that HIS Holy Spirit rests within you. And HE will always remember you because HIS Seal, the Holy Spirit, is living in you and You both belong to HIM. He will redeem you to HIMSELF with HIS Holy Spirit in you. And it is HIS Seal that HE places in you as HIS promise to you, to show you are faithful to HIM without sin, and deserving to live for eternal Life in HIS New Kingdom. HIS Holy Spirit will help us Testify about our Lord Jesus Christ and our relationship with Him by the Holy Spirit of our GOD the Father.

We must Testify to help others understand how much we are loved and cared for by the Holy Spirit of our GOD the Father and through the Spirit of our Lord Jesus Christ.

Chapter 9: Holy Spirit will Testify...You Also Must

- ### Exodus 19 N.I.V.,
  18 Mount Sinai was covered with smoke because the LORD (GOD the Father) descended on it in Fire. The smoke billowed up from it like smoke from a furnace, and the whole mountain trembled violently. 19 As the sound of the trumpet grew louder and louder, Moses spoke, and the Voice of GOD answered him.

- ### Acts 2 N.I.V.,
  1 When the day of Pentecost came, they were all together in one place. 2 Suddenly a sound like the blowing of a violent wind came from Heaven and filled the whole house where they were sitting. 3 They saw what seemed to be tongues of fire that separated and came to rest on each of them. 4 All of them were filled with the Holy Spirit (Anointed) and began to speak in other tongues as the Spirit enabled them.

- ### Ephesians 1:13-14 (NIV)
  13 And you also were included in Christ when you heard the message of Truth, the Gospel of your salvation. When you believed, you were marked in Him with a Seal, the promised Holy Spirit, 14 who is a deposit guaranteeing our inheritance until the redemption of those who are GOD's possession—To the praise of HIS glory.

Now you will know the Word of Truth and the difference of baptism. Do not be confused by the twisted ideas or doctrine of men working for their own selfish desires by confusing the World and making it complicated to become baptized. Believe only in the written Word and the Truth in it, and use it to prove, reprove, and reproach the lies that blind and fool the weak, naive, and double minds.

You only need to believe the Testimony of our GOD the Father concerning HIS Son, our Lord Jesus Christ. And after submitting and committing yourself to our GOD the Father by giving thanks by praying in Spirit that you believe in the NAME of HIS Son, our Lord Jesus Christ; our GOD the Father will send HIS Holy Spirit into you in the NAME of HIS Son, Jesus Christ. That's when you will have left the condemned to stand Holy in Spirit.

Being baptized in water by John the Baptist was only for the repenting of sin. After our Lord Jesus Christ returned to our GOD the Father in Heaven, now we are being baptized by the Holy Spirit and Fire, just like John the Baptist described it.

Being baptized with the Holy Spirit is being "Anointed" with the Holy Spirit to become a Holy Child of our GOD the Father in the NAME of our Lord Jesus Christ with THEM in us, in complete unity. We receive the Holy Spirit that goes out from our GOD the Father into us. Which legitimizes your forgiveness and repentance of all your sins combined, by the power in the Blood Sacrifice of our Lord Jesus Christ that you believe in. And the Holy Spirit is also the Seal of our GOD the Father set in you, that marks you in HIS Son Jesus Christ as belonging to our GOD the Father. Only then, with the help of our Lord Jesus Christ, you will have been made Holy, legitimately sanctified for salvation, and ready for the redemption to eternal Life in HIS Kingdom.

That is the difference between each baptism for their perspective time and purpose. There is no requirement to be submerged in water to receive the Holy Spirit and be saved now. The only first requirement is to believe the Testimony of our GOD the Father in your heart and declare with your mouth that Jesus Christ is your Lord. Yet, if it is your personal desire to be baptized in water, in the NAME of our Lord Jesus Christ to receive the Holy Spirit from our GOD the Father into you, then do it now in

Chapter 9: Holy Spirit will Testify...You Also Must

Spiritual prayer. Do it all in the NAME of our Lord Jesus Christ and giving thanks to our GOD the Father. Then live by the Word of Truth and keep the commands to stay Holy in our Lord Jesus Christ. Live and pray in the Spirit giving thanks to our GOD the Father through our Lord Jesus Christ.

Do not hinder anyone from going to our Lord Jesus Christ and becoming Children of our GOD the Father. And however you decide to submit and commit your personal Spirit to our GOD the Father in the NAME of HIS Son Jesus Christ; as long as you believe in your heart without a doubt, in the Testimony of our GOD the Father, and declare with your mouth that Jesus Christ is your Lord and your Savior and repent your sins to him, then you will receive the Holy Spirit and have our Lord Jesus Christ living in you with eternal Life, in complete unity.

This is the Word, and it is the Truth.

- **Mathew 3:11 (NIV)**
  11 "*I baptize you with water for repentance.* (John the Baptist) *But after me comes One who is more powerful than I, whose sandals I am not worthy to carry. He* (Jesus Christ) *will baptize you with the Holy Spirit and Fire.*

This can only happen to believers of the Word, who believe our GOD the Father sent our Lord Jesus Christ and commit to follow the commands of our Lord Jesus Christ. Only those who present themselves to our Lord Jesus Christ as they are, with all their sins repented can be forgiven.

You must drag all your sins out of the darkness and into the Light, to expose everything about yourself that you truly want to ask our Lord Jesus Christ to forgive you for, and He will not turn you away. Those who go to Him for eternal Life and ask to be forgiven in the NAME of our Lord Jesus Christ will be forgiven to be presented Holy in the sight of our GOD the Father. And they "will not be judged" by our Lord Jesus Christ on the Judgement Day, the Last Day, because there will be no sin, fault, or accusation in them to be judged for. That is what we want for all our Brothers and Sisters being called because it is the will of our GOD the Father and our Lord Jesus Christ. Because we believe only He can forgive us and grant us eternal Life with the Life in Him, and we accept Him to live in unity in us. We will live as the Holy Children of our GOD the Father now in this appointed time on Earth and forever after we are raised up.

When our Lord Jesus Christ sent the Apostles out to continue to baptize in His NAME, after He returned to Heaven and showed Himself alive again to them, they were sent out to baptize believers to receive the Holy Spirit into themselves instantly, right where they were standing or sitting when they first believed. The Apostle Paul, who was not with the original Twelve Apostles before our Lord Jesus Christ returned to Heaven, was Chosen by Him to bring the Gentiles into believing in the Testimony of our GOD the Father. You can repent and receive the Holy Spirit in Spirit prayer in the NAME of our Lord Jesus Christ at anytime, anywhere in your life now, by believing in your heart and proclaiming with your Mouth that our GOD the Father sent our Lord Jesus Christ to be our Savior to reconcile us back to HIMSELF through our Lord Jesus Christ.

If you haven't asked in the NAME of our Lord Jesus Christ for the Holy Spirit, and you believe in Him in your heart without a doubt; then ask our GOD the Father in the NAME of our Lord Jesus Christ to send you HIS Holy Spirit into you to accept Him to lead your Spirit for eternal Life, in complete unity with THEM. And our Lord Jesus Christ will do it for you to glorify our GOD the Father. Exactly as our Lord Jesus Christ teaches us in the Word. That will be the beginning of your inspiration for eternal Life living in the Spirit and your Testimony to tell. That will be the beginning of your testimony about your sanctification and salvation.

Our Lord Jesus Christ sent the Holy Spirit to save a man who was sentenced to be condemned and crucified to death on the cross next to Himself. Because the man spoke and asked our Lord Jesus Christ to

Chapter 9: Holy Spirit will Testify...You Also Must

remember Him, our Lord Jesus Christ told him that he would be in paradise with Him that day. The man acknowledged his sin was wrong of him and believed in our Lord Jesus Christ. There was no water dipping necessary for him to be taken from his crucifix to paradise that day.

The same goes for you and everyone in our day and age. Our Lord Jesus Christ forgave the man on the cross next to Him of all his sins while the man was hanging on the cross; because he repented his own sins on the cross and believed in our Lord Jesus Christ in his heart without doubt. He believed that our Lord Jesus Christ was sent by our GOD the Father and was going back to His Holy Kingdom. And the Holy Spirit of our GOD the Father raised him to be with our Lord Jesus Christ the same way our Lord Jesus Christ was raised up after His death on the cross, and they were both in Paradise that day.

- **Luke 23:39-43 (NIV)**
  *39 One of the criminals who hung there hurled insults at Him: "Aren't you the Messiah? Save yourself and us!" 40 But the other criminal rebuked him. "Don't you fear GOD," he said, "since you are under the same sentence? 41 We are punished justly, for we are getting what our deeds deserve. But this MAN (Jesus Christ) has done nothing wrong." 42 Then he said, "Jesus, remember me when You come into Your Kingdom." 43 Jesus answered him, **"Truly I tell you**, Today you will be with Me in Paradise."*

It was after our Lord Jesus Christ was raised from the dead that He commanded the Apostles to baptize in the NAME of Jesus Christ the Son, the Holy Spirit, and our GOD the Father and to teach others to keep the commands that He taught them; because it was possible at that time after He was raised from the dead and returned to Heaven to ask our GOD the Father to send His Holy Spirit into anyone who believes in Him and our GOD the Father. And our GOD the Father glorified Him with the Authority to send HIS Holy Spirit into anyone who believes in Him and goes to Him for eternal Life.

- **Mathew 28:19-20 (NIV)**
  19 Therefore go and make disciples of all nations, baptizing them in the NAME of the Father and of the Son and of the Holy Spirit, 20 and teaching them to obey everything I have commanded you. And surely, I am with you always, to the very end of the age."

Receiving the Holy Spirit into you is a miracle sent from our GOD the Father in the NAME of our Lord Jesus Christ. That makes us One, in complete unity with THEM. And believing in Him is your personal Spirit living by His commands in the written Word and following the guidance of the Holy Spirit in you. That is how your personal Spirit with the Holy Spirit will testify together.

Without living by the guidance of the Holy Spirit, people are living by the desires of the flesh to their death. But we as believers in the Word of Truth understand that we belong to our GOD the Father in this Body-Temple in complete unity no matter where we are in this appointed time in our life, even if we are wrongly accused and put in prison or treated harshly, we are there to glorify our GOD the Father in the NAME of our Lord Jesus Christ for HIS purpose and grace. We shall not waiver from the narrow path in shame, no! What we shall do is continue to walk in Spirit on our appointed path to glorify our GOD the Father every moment of our lives. For believers in our Lord Jesus Christ, we know He gives us the Holy Spirit for eternal Life, and we will be redeemed, raised up by the Holy Spirit at our appointed time.

- **Galatians 6:7-8 (NIV)**

Chapter 9: Holy Spirit will Testify...You Also Must

7 Do not be deceived: GOD cannot be mocked. A man reaps what he sows. 8...Whoever sows to please the Spirit, (Holy Spirit) from the Spirit will reap eternal Life.

- **Galatians 5:16-26 (NIV)**

  16 So I say, walk by the Spirit, and you will not gratify the desires of the flesh. 17 For the flesh desires what is contrary to the Spirit, and the Spirit what is contrary to the flesh. They conflict with each other, so that you are not to do whatever you want. 18 But if you are led by the Spirit, you are not under the law. (Old Testament) *19 The acts of the flesh are obvious: sexual immorality, impurity and debauchery; 20 idolatry and witchcraft; hatred, discord, jealousy, fits of rage, selfish ambition, dissensions, factions 21 and envy; drunkenness, orgies, and the like. I warn you, as I did before, that those who live like this will not inherit the Kingdom of GOD. 22 But the fruit of the Spirit is love, joy, peace, forbearance, kindness, goodness, faithfulness, 23 gentleness and self-control. Against such things there is no law. 24 Those who belong to Christ Jesus have crucified the flesh with its passions and desires. 25 Since we live by the Spirit, let us keep in step with the Spirit. 26 Let us not become conceited, provoking, and envying each other.*

- **2 Timothy 1:7-10 (NIV)**

  7 For the Spirit GOD gave us does not make us timid, but gives us power, love and self- discipline. 8 So do not be ashamed of the Testimony about our Lord or of me His prisoner. (Apostle Paul) *Rather, join with me in suffering for the Gospel, by the power of GOD. 9 HE has saved us and called us to a Holy Life—Not because of anything we have done but because of HIS own purpose and grace. This grace was given us in Christ Jesus before the beginning of time, 10 but it has now been revealed through the appearing of our Savior Christ Jesus, who has destroyed death and has brought Life and Immortality (eternal Life) to light through the Gospel.*

Our GOD the Father loves us continuously, day and night, for loving HIS Son, our Lord Jesus Christ. Immortality was intended to be in humankind before the beginning of time. Then it was taken away from our bodies on Earth by our GOD the Father for the transgression against HIS commands by our Ancient Ancestors (Adam and Eve).

Our personal Spirit is made immortal and can only be condemned by the authority of our GOD the Father. But HE promised to redeem us and has given us eternal life through our Lord Jesus Christ, to believe in and follow to our Day of Redemption back to our GOD the Father. This is the time we live in, where we are saved from judgment. And now, "we" must Testify to others about our Lord Jesus Christ, to help them grow up in the Word of Truth and live in the Spirit as our Brothers and Sisters having the Life of our Lord Jesus Christ in themselves with the love of our only true GOD the Father in complete unity.

Chapter 9: Holy Spirit will Testify...You Also Must

AND THIS IS OUR PRAYER:

We pray to You, our GOD the Father, for the wisdom and courage to speak Your Word from our Hearts and our Mouths to glorify You and our Lord Jesus Christ. We ask for Your Holy Spirit to help us give our Testimony to anyone who is seeking Your love to know the Truth in Your Word.

Give us the strength we need from Your Word of Truth to Testify about our Lord Jesus Christ. And by the power of His NAME Jesus Christ, and in the baptism of Your Holy Spirit and Fire, our Brothers and Sisters will be saved out of the fire of condemnation by Your will for their salvation.

We pray to ask You in the NAME of Your Son, our Lord Jesus Christ.

Chapter 10: *He Did Go… He Does Send*

John 16:1-7 NIV

1 "All this I have told you so that you will not fall away.

2 They will put you out of the Synagogue; in fact, the time is coming when anyone who kills you will think they are offering a service to GOD.

3 They will do such things because they have not known the Father or Me.

4 I have told you this, so that when the time comes you will remember that I warned you about them. I did not tell you this from the beginning because I was with you,

5 but now I am going to HIM (GOD the Father) who sent Me. (Jesus Christ) None of you asks Me, 'Where are you going?'

6 Rather, you are filled with grief because I have said these things.

7 But **very truly I tell you**, it is for your good that I am going away. Unless I go away, (Holy Spirit) the Advocate will not come.

❖ **Notice:**

Chapter 10: He Did Go...He Does Send

Our Lord Jesus Christ said, "All this I have told you so you will not fall away." Letting them know in advance what was going to happen proved that the Holy Spirit of our GOD the Father will be with them and help them keep the commands and that includes doing what we are compelled by the Holy Spirit to do and say to help others reconcile with our GOD the Father.

Our GOD the Father sends HIS Holy Spirit into all believers after our Lord Jesus Christ returned to ask our GOD the Father to send HIS Holy Spirit into us, to help us stay Holy. This is just one example of how the Holy Spirit will tell us things we need to hear in advance, what is to come. (Our Future) You may see things in advance in a split second telling you what you will see, and you will know what you must do to change the events to your favor as needed when you notice the vision or event is taking place. Then take corrective action and you will be amazed at your ability to manage problems with the help of the Holy Spirit of God that has no fear in you.

What you can expect, maybe a change in a relationship with someone, danger, a hardship to beware of, to take quick action, or to get ready to teach the message of the Gospel to someone in need to hear the Word of Truth for their sanctification. No matter what it will be to keep the peace and glorify our GOD the Father and strengthen your faith in HIM. The ones you help may become your Brothers or Sisters who will cross over from death to eternal Life with all their family to be with you and our Lord Jesus Christ in the glorious presence of our GOD the Father, in the New Kingdom, on the New Earth, conjoined with a New Heaven.

Help wake up the Children of our GOD the Father with the Word of Truth that speaks from your heart into their hearts. But it is a true feeling with a purpose that the Holy Spirit tells you to act upon with a purpose in the interest of others. So, you can expect yourself to be prepared by Him for anything you need to do living in Spirit to glorify our GOD the Father in the NAME of our Lord Jesus Christ. You will be called to help turn a situation into a better one. Nothing is left to chance; we will be warned for our own good. We must keep in step with the Holy Spirit when we live by the Spirit and do what He says we should do for our own good to help others and ourselves.

It is for your own good to take advantage of every Choice that He will guide you to for the opportunity to edify our lives to reconcile ourselves and others to know our GOD the Father. It is your responsibility as HIS Holy Child to introduce our Brothers and Sisters to know THEM for eternal Life. You know the Way, the Truth, and the Life because you were called to know it, to help others know it with the help of our Lord Jesus Christ and the guidance of the Holy Spirit living in you.

Remember, our Lord Jesus Christ is telling the Holy Spirit exactly what He wants you to hear, know, do, and speak; and the Holy Spirit repeats it to you, nothing more, nothing less while He reminds you of the Word of Truth that you learned.

- **John 16:13-14 (NIV)**
  13 But when He, the Spirit of Truth, comes, He will guide you into all the Truth. He will not speak on His own; He will speak only what He hears, and He will tell you what is yet to come. 14 He will glorify Me (Jesus Christ) because it is from Me that He will receive what He will make known to you.

Now you know that our Lord Jesus Christ is always with you; helping you by speaking to you through the Holy Spirit of our GOD the Father. Our GOD the Father hears the Groans, which is the Voice of HIS Holy Spirit speaking from your heart, what you need and want to ask of HIM. That is how HIS Holy Spirit guides your Spirit from within you. The Holy Spirit that our GOD the Father gives to us, is because our Lord Jesus Christ asked for that of HIM for us. Therefore, our GOD the Father sends HIS Holy Spirit out from HIMSELF, in the NAME of our Lord Jesus Christ, who asked for it from HIM because you know His will is

Chapter 10: He Did Go...He Does Send

for us to have eternal Life. Our Lord Jesus Christ made it clear that He would ask our GOD the Father to send us HIS Holy Spirit when He returned to our GOD the Father. And He also made it clear that we must worship our GOD the Father while we pray in Spirit and ask of HIM on our own behalf, to glorify HIM, in the NAME of HIS Son our Lord Jesus Christ. This proves that you honor HIS Son our Lord Jesus Christ the same as you honor our GOD the Father who sent HIS Son for our salvation and that you believe the Testimony of our GOD the Father that HE has given about our Lord Jesus Christ.

HE has already established the Choice for us to accept eternal Life in our Mortal Bodies now, by having the Spirit of our Lord Jesus Christ living in our Body-Temple now. Our GOD the Father loves us in every way we can believe what eternal love is. He always establishes our steps to get us where HE needs us to be. And the Decision to believe HIS Testimony and accept HIS Covenant for eternal Life from HIM is the first step towards HIM, which means HE miraculously blesses us with eternal Life on the very first step we take towards Him. Therefore, we are called to live a Holy Life in complete unity with THEM from the very first moment we believe and start living by the New Covenant. We must Decide to accept HIS Gift of Life to cross over from condemnation living by the flesh to eternal Life living by the Spirit having our Lord Jesus Christ with us.

Our Lord Jesus Christ is the Word of Life, and the Spirit of eternal Life is in Him. He was created by our GOD the Father with the Authority to give us eternal Life by our believing the Testimony of our GOD the Father concerning His Son, our Lord Jesus Christ. HIS Choice for us to have eternal Life has been given to us with HIS New Covenant of the Spirit, which surpasses the glory of the Old Covenant, the written law of Moses that brought death. Because we cannot achieve the Righteous Requirement of living by the Old Covenant without having our Lord Jesus Christ.

The Old Covenant places a veil over our hearts and faces every time it is read. The Old Covenant was made transitory for the people of that time, written in stone or ink. It was made to "pass away" for a New Covenant that does give us eternal Life by the Law of the Spirit. That New Covenant of the Spirit of Life has been fulfilled by the Righteousness in our Lord Jesus Christ for our salvation. It has been the will of our GOD the Father for us to have eternal Life since the beginning of time and it is the will of our Lord Jesus Christ to do the will of our GOD the Father for us.

The New Covenant brings us Life through our Lord Jesus Christ, who fulfills all things by His Righteousness that we need in us to meet the Righteous Requirement to have eternal Life starting within our Mortal Bodies, which is our Body-Temple where the Holy Spirit of our GOD the Father rests within us with our personal Spirit and the Spirit of our Lord Jesus Christ in complete unity. Believing in this is to have our Lord Jesus Christ for the crossing over from death to eternal Life now.

This is the Word, and it is the Truth.

By having our Lord Jesus Christ in us, we have eternal Life that He brings into us with the Spirit of Himself to be with us in complete unity. Only by Him is the veil of the Old Covenant removed so that everyone may see the Truth to know the difference between the Old Covenant that brought death and the New Covenant which brings eternal Life of the Spirit which was given to us by our GOD the Father through our Lord Jesus Christ.

We are now living in the age and the appointed time of the New Covenant that is living in us. It is written in our hearts and frees us from the death of the law of the Old Covenant that has passed away. It is difficult for those who followed the Old Covenant to accept this until they experience the effects of living in complete unity and all the blessings that come with the New Covenant. It's not our Choice to have created this change in Covenants, it is the will of our GOD the Father who has made this choice for us, to give us a way out from condemnation, doom, and destruction. It's only our Decision to accept HIS gift of eternal Life. And now we are never alone living in Spirit; we live with the Holy Spirit of our GOD the Father and the Spirit of His Son, our Lord Jesus Christ.

Chapter 10: He Did Go...He Does Send

There is a spiritual change of righteousness that is made within us and that makes us Holy in this appointed time. Once it's done in you and you know it without a doubt, you will know that you have all the help you need from them to carry out your commands in your life. Our Lord Jesus Christ will help you carry them out according to the will of our GOD the Father and according to your faith in THEM.

Now you know the difference of the Old Covenant law, which could not bring Life, only death, and that it was made transitory. And the New Covenant Law of the Spirit that was made to bring eternal Life with our Lord Jesus Christ within us. Because He is eternal Life in us, we become eternal Life in Him by living in complete unity with THEM. All we must do is accept and believe in the New Covenant, which is believing in the Testimony of our GOD the Father and keeping His commands to receive THEM into our heart for eternal Life.

This is the Word, and it is the Truth.

_____

- **2 Corinthians 3:2-18 (NIV)**
  2 You yourselves are our Letter, written on our hearts, known and read by everyone. 3 You show that you are a letter from Christ, the result of our Ministry, written not with ink but with the Spirit of the living GOD, not on tablets of stone but on tablets of human hearts. 4 Such confidence we have through Christ before GOD. 5 Not that we are competent in ourselves to claim anything for ourselves, but our competence comes from GOD. 6 HE has made us competent as Ministers of a New Covenant not of the letter but of the Spirit; for the letter kills, but the Spirit gives Life. (New Covenant) 7 Now if the ministry (Old Covenant) that brought death, which was engraved in letters on stone, came with glory, so that the Israelites could not look steadily at the face of Moses because of its glory, transitory though it was, 8 will not the (New Covenant) Ministry of the Spirit be even more glorious? 9 If the (Old

Covenant) ministry that brought condemnation was glorious, how much more glorious is the (New Covenant) *Ministry that brings righteousness! 10 For what was glorious* (Old Covenant) *has no glory now in comparison with the* (New Covenant) *surpassing glory. 11 And if* (Old Covenant) *what was transitory came with glory, how much greater is the* (New Covenant) *glory of that which lasts! 12 Therefore, since we have such a hope, we are very bold. 13 We are not like Moses, who would put a veil over his face to prevent the Israelites from seeing the end of what was passing away. 14 But their minds were made dull, for to this day the same veil remains when the "Old Covenant" is read. It has not been removed, because only in Christ is it taken away. 15 Even to this day when Moses is read, a veil covers their hearts. 16 But whenever anyone turns to the Lord,* (New Covenant) *the veil is taken away. 17 Now the Lord is the Spirit, and where the Spirit of the Lord is, there is freedom. 18 And we all, who with unveiled faces contemplate the Lord's glory, are being transformed into His image with ever-increasing glory, which comes from the Lord, who is the Spirit.*

――――

Now you know what the New Covenant is, and that the New Covenant is for anyone that turns to our Lord Jesus Christ for Life because we must have our Lord Jesus Christ living in unity within us to have eternal Life by the New Covenant of our GOD the Father reconciling everything to HIMSELF.

Learn to trust our Lord Jesus Christ with your instincts, and your feelings from your heart, when you are living with His Spirit and the Holy Spirit who is guiding you in your Life on a straight path to salvation with eternal Life now, then after we are raised up for redemption to be with our GOD the Father. Ask questions and you shall receive the answers from our Lord Jesus Christ. Just have faith and patience until He speaks to you when He wants you to know, in His time, in His Grand Plan for

Chapter 10: He Did Go...He Does Send

your Life.

The Spirit of our Lord Jesus Christ is also living in you, so you can live in peace without fear of anything because He is with you, and He loves you. Our Lord Jesus Christ has in Him all the power of our GOD the Father dwelling in Him that was given to Him by our GOD the Father to help us at His own discretion. He will answer, empower, and remind you at the perfect time depending on your abilities and faith to do what you need to do to be safe and successful in your Life.

Our Lord Jesus Christ was created divine in His nature and our GOD the Father is pleased to have HIS fullness dwelling in Him. In the NAME of our Lord Jesus Christ be bold with speaking the Truth in the message, which is the Testimony of our GOD the Father, while doing your deeds to glorify our GOD the Father.

- **Colossians 1:19-20 (NIV)**

    19 For GOD was pleased to have all HIS fullness dwell in Him, (Jesus Christ) *20 and through Him to reconcile to HIMSELF all things,* (GOD the Father) *whether things on Earth or things in Heaven, by making peace through His blood,* (Jesus Christ) *shed on the Cross.*

- **2 Timothy 1:7 (NIV)**

    7 For the Spirit GOD gave us does not make us timid, but gives us power, love, and self-discipline.

Be cautious of evil, it is wise to shun evil by living in the Spirit and remembering the Word of Truth to prove your righteousness and love for our Lord Jesus Christ. Be grateful for our Lord Jesus Christ that at least you are blessed to know the truth to prepare yourself and fearlessly deal with any life problems rationally.

It is truly a miracle when we feel it in our heart, every time the Holy Spirit is guiding our Spirit. We feel it without a doubt every time when we live to please the Holy Spirit of our living GOD the Father that is within us. Our Lord Jesus Christ is our friend, and His Spirit is dwelling in us with the Holy Spirit. We feel His love, sometimes so powerful it makes us cry tears of joy. That is His joy that brings us peace that He gives in us. Be humble and glorify our Lord Jesus Christ by praying in His NAME while giving thanks to our GOD the Father in spiritual prayer for being there for you; and for having mercy on your soul with HIS love.

"Everything happens for a reason" is a true statement. You will learn to live by that statement and track all the little changes in things that will happen in your Life to bring you to the point of revelations, time and time again. When living with the Holy Spirit those reasons are revealed to you in everything you do. You may be given a small hint that your prayers are heard, then later be given evidence that your prayers were answered. Your feelings and warnings are for your protection and to temper your faith stronger in your Spirit, which is why the reasons are revealed to us why certain things have happened in your life. And then your mind will have clarity to the fact that our GOD the Father is always helping HIS Children in their Holy Life at all times. That is our Testimony so, we can Testify about the Word of Truth to others with our own Testimony of how living in complete unity is truly miraculous. And you can Testify how each step that was established for you placed you in the exact places you needed to be for your protection by the Ones that live within you with more love than you can imagine.

Our GOD the Father knows your true limitations of what you can and can't manage, and what Choices to establish for you to follow in your life, because HE is delivering HIS blessings to you by HIS design for your own good for your salvation and faith in HIM. He has provided Choices for you ever since you Decided to be guided by HIS Holy Spirit. Pay close attention to HIM, to keep up with HIS Holy Spirit because your Life depends on you living in complete unity while trusting in the

Chapter 10: He Did Go...He Does Send

Lord Jesus Christ helping you. Do not do anything in words or deeds without asking our GOD the Father for help to do HIS will while giving thanks to HIM praying in Spirit through our Lord Jesus Christ.

The Holy Spirit will guide you in this World to get you to where you need to be, to glorify our GOD the Father at every opportunity to make HIM known to others. That is how we stay in HIS love by following HIS commands in our Holy Life every day. HE will even help you pick your friends for you and cut off the ones you cannot have in your life at that time. HE does this to protect your heart, mind, and soul to help keep you pure and Holy for our Lord Jesus Christ, so on the Last Day you will be presented to HIM Holy in HIS sight.

- **1 Corinthians 10:12-13 N.I.V.**
  12 So, if you think you are standing firm, be careful that you don't fall! 13 No temptation has overtaken you except what is common to Mankind. And GOD is faithful, HE will not let you be tempted beyond what you can bear. But when you are tempted, HE will also provide a way out so that you can endure it.

You just need to be patient, and trust HIM unconditionally, and enjoy HIS fitting you into HIS Grand Plan that includes blessing you more than you can imagine. No matter how this appointed time ends for HIS Holy Children, our GOD the Father will restore each one of us and make us imperishable for eternal Life with HIM.

- **Proverbs 3:5-8 (NIV)**
  5 Trust in the LORD (GOD the Father) with all your heart and lean not on your own understanding; 6 in all your ways submit to HIM, and HE will make your paths straight. 7 Do not be wise in your own eyes, fear the LORD and shun evil. 8 This will

bring health to your body and nourishment to your bones.

Because the Apostles were warned, they did not lose faith or fall away as our Lord Jesus Christ said, and they were able to give us their Testimony by the Gospel of our Lord Jesus Christ in the New Testament containing the New Covenant made for us to believe. Our Lord Jesus Christ reassured us that He will have the Authority to have the Holy Spirit sent to whoever believes in Him. But only after He returned and asked for it from the One (GOD the Father) who sent Him; and that is, ask our GOD the Father to send us HIS Holy Spirit into us. And He did return, and He does send the Holy Spirit for us to be baptized with and cross over from death to Life at that time.

Once you believe and submit and commit yourself to our GOD the Father you are HIS Child forever. And HIS Son, our Lord Jesus Christ will watch over you and protect you forever without a doubt. Remember who you are, as a living Spirit Child of our GOD the Father because you are Heir to HIS Kingdom in Heaven with our Lord Jesus Christ. You must continue to listen to your heart and practice how to follow HIS Holy Spirit in you. He is telling you what our Lord Jesus Christ wants you to say and do to tune you up to His speed to recognize what you are being told.

- ### Ephesians 1:14-14 (NIV)
    13 And you also were included in Christ when you heard the message of Truth, the Gospel of your salvation. When you believed, (Jesus Christ) you were marked in Him with a Seal, the promised Holy Spirit, 14 who is a deposit guaranteeing our inheritance until the redemption of those who are GOD'S possession— To the praise of HIS glory.

The Holy Spirit will speak on your behalf even if you do not know what to

Chapter 10: He Did Go...He Does Send

pray for. Our GOD the Father searches your heart where the Life of your blood cries out to Him; where everything you want to say comes from before you can think of how to put it into words.

Have courage and don't worry too much about that, you will get better at listening and watching for signs over time. Besides, the Holy Spirit knows you better than yourself since He doesn't sleep and will speak on your behalf as needed without you knowing what happened until it is revealed to you. And the Holy Spirit living in you knows the desires of your heart and cries out to our GOD the Father for you. Keep your heart pure by protecting it with the Word of Truth and reject every immoral thought that may cross your mind in the NAME of our Lord Jesus Christ, so that your heart will remain in the love of our Lord Jesus Christ and our GOD the Father.

The Holy Spirit will Groan what you need from your heart when He is telling our GOD the Father everything that you wish for in your heart before you can think to know what you need. Then HE will know before you know what you want to say in your mind in prayer before you speak. Be confident and bold in your faith, you are a Child that belongs to our GOD the Father the creator of you. Have no doubt that HE hears every word you speak because our GOD the Father listens to those with HIS Holy Spirit living in them.

You can say this yourself and proclaim it with your Testimony to others: "I am a Child of our GOD the Father and the eternal Life of HIS Son, my Lord Jesus Christ, is living in me. And the Holy Spirit of our GOD the Father is also living in me, guiding my Spirit to do HIS will."

That coincides with the Testimony of our GOD the Father.

- **1 John 5:11-12 (NIV)**
  *11 And this is the Testimony: **GOD has given us eternal Life, and this Life is in HIS Son. 12 Whoever has the***

Son has Life; whoever does not have the Son of GOD does not have Life.

―――

We live in our Spirit, with HIS Holy Spirit, and the Spirit of our Lord Jesus Christ within us. The same Holy Spirit that comes out of our GOD the Father and that raised our Lord Jesus Christ from the dead. And it is the same Holy Spirit that will raise us up to a new imperishable Spirit Body when it is our appointed time.

―――

- Romans 8:11 (NIV)
   11 And if the Spirit of HIM (GOD the Father) *who raised Jesus from the dead is living in you, He* (Holy Spirit) *who raised Christ from the dead will also give life to your Mortal Bodies, because of HIS* (GOD the Father) *Spirit who lives in you.*

―――

The Holy Spirit of our GOD the Father raised our Lord Jesus Christ from the dead and is now living in us and will raise us from the dead too. Our Lord Jesus Christ has returned to our GOD the Father; and our GOD the Father did send HIS Holy Spirit out from HIMSELF, in the NAME of HIS Son Jesus Christ, and into us to live in everyone that believes in our Lord Jesus Christ. They both intercede for us to our GOD the Father. The Holy Spirit with Wordless Groans from our heart, and the Spirit of our Lord Jesus Christ is atoning for our sins at the Right Hand of our GOD the Father in Heaven.

―――

- Romans 8:26-27 (NIV)
   26 In the same way, the Spirit helps us in our weakness. We do not know what we ought to pray for, but the Spirit Himself

intercedes for us through Wordless Groans. <u>27</u> *And HE who searches our hearts* (GOD the Father) *knows the mind of the Holy Spirit, because the Spirit intercedes for GOD'S people in accordance with the will of GOD.*

- ## Romans 8:34 (NIV)
    <u>34</u> *Who then is the one who condemns? No one. Christ Jesus who died—More than that, who was raised to Life—is at the Right Hand of GOD and is also interceding for us.*

As believers in the Word of Truth, we have crossed over from death to Life in complete unity; therefore, we are no longer conflicted about our salvation while we live in our Lord Jesus Christ as Children of our GOD the Father because we are no longer condemned, awaiting doom and destruction, as we continue to walk in the Spirit so we will not be judged to see any shame on the Last Day.

Now that we know that we live by the guidance of the Holy Spirit in us and that our Lord Jesus Christ did have Him sent into us, be faithful and do not say or do anything without the guidance of the Holy Spirit in the NAME of our Lord Jesus Christ, while you pray in Spirit to give thanks to our GOD the Father. THEY give you the Choices in your life and establish your steps for you to help keep you stay on the narrow path to walk Holy in Spirit now and for eternal Life.

- ## Colossians 3:17 (NIV)
    <u>17</u> *And whatever you do, whether in word or deed, do it all in the NAME of the Lord Jesus, giving thanks to GOD the Father through Him.* (Jesus Christ)

"We are not our own, we belong to the One and only Living GOD the Father." And THEY will come to us and make THEIR home with us.

──

- ### 1 Corinthians 6:19 (NIV)
    19 Do you not know that your Bodies are Temples of the Holy Spirit, who is in you, whom you have received from GOD? You are not your own.

──

In everything that you say and do, follow the Choices and steps established by our GOD the Father through HIS Son and HIS Holy Spirit, that is in your Body-Temple as One with your personal Spirit, to keep your personal Spirit Holy now and for eternal Life. When you appear with our Lord Jesus Christ in Heaven, He will present you, Holy, in the presence of our GOD the Father, and HIS Holy Spirit will Testify by His presence with you, that you are HIS Child for eternal Life.

This is the Word, and it is the Truth.

Chapter 10: He Did Go...He Does Send

AND THIS IS OUR PRAYER:

We pray in Spirit to thank You, our GOD the Father, for sending Your Holy Spirit into our Body-Temple to guide us and teach us Your Word of Truth. And for Your protection by the NAME of Your Son, our Lord Jesus Christ. May we have peace and wisdom to help the weak learn how to live by Your Holy Spirit to know You, our GOD the Father, and Your Son our Lord Jesus Christ who You sent to us for our salvation.

We ask in the NAME of Your Son, our Lord Jesus Christ.

Chapter 11: He Makes It Known

John 16:8-15 NIV

8 "When He (Holy Spirit) comes, He will prove the World to be in the wrong about Sin, and Righteousness, and Judgement:

9 About Sin, because people do not believe in Me (Jesus Christ);

10 about Righteousness, because I am going to the Father, where you can see Me no longer;

11 and about Judgement, because (Satan) the prince of this World now stands condemned.

12 "I have much more to say to you, more than you can now bear.

13 But when He, the Spirit of Truth comes, He will guide you into all the Truth. He will not speak on His own; He will speak only what He hears, and He will tell you what is yet to come.

14 He will glorify Me (Jesus Christ) because it is from Me that He will receive what He will make known to you.

15 All that belongs to the Father is Mine. That is why I said the Spirit will receive from Me (Jesus Christ) What He will make known to you.

❖ Notice:

Our Lord Jesus Christ will speak to us through the Holy Spirit, who will make known to us what He wants us to know. Even the future in our

Chapter 12: Rejoice in the NAME, Jesus Christ

Life. He will tell you what you need to know in advance to make you stronger in faith when it happens.

The Holy Spirit lives in you, knows you, and knows how to make you understand what THEY want you to know for your own good. Our GOD the Father Spoke HIS Words and did HIS miraculous works through our Lord Jesus Christ to make the Word known to us. By having the Holy Spirit of our GOD the Father in us, we are living in complete unity. Glorifying our GOD the Father is by being fruitful by believing in your Heart and proclaiming with your Mouth that our Lord Jesus Christ is your Lord, believing the Testimony of our GOD the Father, believing and keeping the commands that our Lord Jesus Christ taught us, believing that we must teach others how-to know and accept HIM and our Lord Jesus Christ so they may enter eternal Life with THEM in their Mortal Body-Temple to live Holy in Spirit now as Holy Children in HIS Sight.

We are expected to help others learn about our Lord Jesus Christ to save them in the World by sharing the Gospel, the written Word, the Testimony of our GOD the Father, and the New Covenant, to help reconcile everyone who is being called to our GOD the Father through our Lord Jesus Christ for eternal Life.

- **John 4:23-24 (NIV)**
    23 Yet a time is coming and has now come when the True worshippers will worship the Father in the Spirit and in Truth, for they are the kind of worshippers the Father seeks. 24 GOD is Spirit, and HIS worshippers must worship in the Spirit and in Truth."

Believers have Decided to live in the Spirit that we were born with, as we speak the Truth that we learned in the Word, and have a Spirit fellowship with the Holy Spirit, and also with the Spirit of our Lord Jesus Christ living in us, in complete unity.

INSPIRATION FOR YOUR ETERNAL LIFE

- **1 Thessalonians 4:7-8 (NIV)**
  7 For GOD did not call us to be impure, but to live a Holy Life. 8 Therefore, anyone who "rejects this instruction does not reject a human being but GOD, the very GOD who gives you HIS Holy Spirit.

Believers are living Holy with THEM in the Spirit today and now; and we will be remembered on the Last Day. We will be redeemed and given eternal Life with imperishable Spirit Bodies. The ones living in unity with our Lord Jesus Christ will be raised up with the Holy Spirit, first the Holy ones in their graves that have died will be called up to our Lord Jesus Christ, and those living Holy in unity will meet them in the clouds.

- **1 Thessalonians 4:16-17 (NIV)**
  16 For the Lord Himself will come down from Heaven, with a Loud Command, with the Voice of the Archangel and with the Trumpet Call of GOD, and the Dead in Christ will rise first. 17 After that, we who are still alive, and are left, will be caught up together with them in the clouds to meet the Lord in the air. And so, we will be with the Lord forever.

You must accept to have our Lord Jesus Christ in you now, to have His eternal Life in you now and after your Body-Temple passes away to be raised up to life again. And that Life is in our Lord Jesus Christ living in you and giving your personal Spirit Life because you believe in Him, by believing the Testimony of our GOD the Father concerning Him. When He calls us up to Himself in the clouds, the Holy Spirit of our GOD the Father will put the power in us to raise us up to Him in the clouds.

We will all bow our knees at the Throne of our Lord Jesus Christ when

Chapter 12: Rejoice in the NAME, Jesus Christ

we see Him in His glory. And those that are His will be given their reward for their good and Holy commitment to Him, which they will be given the Crown of eternal Life, also called the Crown of Righteousness and the Crown of Glory. That is to glorify those who lived and worshipped in the Spirit and did HIS good deeds while in their Body-Temple on Earth.

Those that are condemned now and reject to believe in Him and our GOD the Father, will be judged. They will die for the bad things they did on Earth, while living by their sinful desires of flesh, in their body. They will be raised up for judgment to have the condemnation of their spirit finally executed. After their body of flesh dies, they will have a Second and Final Death, which is the execution of their personal Spirit. The same execution awaits all those "evil spirits" that are condemned now. It's the same condemnation that Satan and all the wicked know that there is an appointed time that their execution will take place without fail. Those who failed to obey our Lord Jesus Christ now stand condemned. They will all be executed for the evil acts of their own desires to live in sin that they refuse to repent.

- **2 Corinthians 5:10 (NIV)**
  10 For we must all appear before the Judgement Seat of Christ, so that each of us may receive what is due us for the "things done while in the body", whether good "or" bad.

- **2 Corinthians 5:20-21 (NIV)**
  20 We are therefore Christ's Ambassadors, as though GOD were making His Appeal through us. We implore you on Christ's behalf: Be reconciled to GOD. 21 GOD made Him, (Jesus Christ) who had no sin, to be sin for us, so that in Him we might become the Righteousness of GOD.

This is the Word, and it is the Truth.

The personal Decision for everyone now is to decide to accept the gift of eternal Life living in the Spirit to know and live with our Lord Jesus Christ and GOD the Father. Or, to remain condemned by rejecting to live in the Spirit with THEM, which is to remain living in vain with sin by the desires of the flesh, resulting in the judgment to be condemned to their doom and destruction. And the result for those that reject GOD by that Decision will be for their spirit to be consigned to the place reserved for them to be finally executed out of existence in the Second Death for their condemnation. Just like worthless vine branches that are detached from the vine and withered to then be collected to be destroyed in the fire, since there is no need for vine branches that will not produce good fruit.

They stand condemned, as Satan now stands condemned, and their final execution will be their appointed time of destruction. Resulting in the nonexistence of all those evil and non-believing spirits, which is the same as what Satan the "evil one" and his disgraced followers will receive. Their names will be blotted out from the Book of Life, and they will lose their place in Heaven because there will be no place found for them in Heaven. Those who have our Lord Jesus Christ in unity on the Last Day are not afraid to see Him in His glory at His Throne because we will not be judged or see shame. We have Him in us now and forever. We know Him and we love Him already, therefore, He will love us in Heaven at His Throne because we are One with Him. There is no reason to judge His Children when He knows we are already living Holy without sin.

Our GOD the Father is perfect and divine; HE had no beginning and has no end. He is eternal and is referred to as The Eternal One. He referred to HIMSELF as I AM. He always was and is and will be for eternal Life as our GOD the Creator. He is called the Father meaning the One who brings anything into being created, the origin and source of all power for creation. That includes HIS first-born creation, HIS Son, our Lord Jesus Christ. HIS Son is the Christ. And all things were created through Him, by the source of power and authority from our GOD the Father.

This is how we distinguish between THEM is, the created Son is Servant

Chapter 12: Rejoice in the NAME, Jesus Christ

to our Creator, ours and His own GOD and LORD, who is everyone's GOD. And the WORD of Life is our Lord Jesus Christ, who is also referred to as the WORD, or the Anointed One, which means the Christ. He is also referred to as the Lamb of GOD or the Lamb, which means He was the Final Sacrificial Lamb that was sacrificed once and for all who repent sin and believe in Him. He also proclaims about Himself, that our GOD the Father is Greater than Himself. And that no one is good except GOD alone. And we, also as creations of our GOD the Father, must also submit and commit ourselves as servants to our GOD the Father through believing in His Son, our Lord Jesus Christ. The same way He submitted and committed Himself to our GOD the Father.

In the beginning of creation, our Lord Jesus Christ was created first by our GOD the Father, and He was created also perfect and divine in nature as a Spirit, also called the WORD of GOD or the WORD. And He was made in the divine image by having the same nature as our GOD the Father, who is Eternal Spirit and Love HIMSELF. He was with our GOD the Father in Heaven as HIS first and only born Son. So, just like He Testified in the Gospel, He saw the creation of the Earth, He was born before the World was made. And He saw the day Lucifer (Satan) Fell like Lightning from Heaven to Earth. The following angels of Satan, referred to as his angels fought along with him and were also extracted from Heaven with Satan, by the Arch Angel Michael and his Angels who were commanded to cast them all down to Earth with Satan the devil.

His only begotten Son, also called, the Word of GOD, His Anointed One, His Christ, His Chosen One, was given a NAME of power, which was also created by our GOD the Father. And that NAME is destined to be above all other Names invoked in Heaven, and Earth, and Under Earth forever. And by that NAME, the NAME of our Lord Jesus Christ, we are protected from evil. And there was nothing after His Creation that wasn't made through Him, by the power of our GOD the Father.

In the text John 1, translated in an English language bible text, the WORD "was God" has the meaning, was divine in nature, in the original scroll text. It is written differently in the original text when referring to our GOD the Father, the way our Lord Jesus Christ had said we must know our GOD the Father and worship HIM as the only GOD of all. That translation can be misleading or mistaken by a reader in English because the word "god" itself has several meanings in the English Language.

Do not be confused, learn the Word of Truth and believe what is consistent in it. Our Lord Jesus Christ tells us that our GOD the Father is greater than Himself the SON. Because He never said that He was GOD and He never, ever claimed equality with our GOD, His Father which means His Creator, any more than anyone else on Earth or in Heaven can think to claim equality with our GOD the Father. Anyone or anything that claims equality with our GOD the Father is a "Liar", because they are referring to our Lord Jesus Christ by a Lie. That is a sin and deceitfulness that causes division and leads disciples astray from the Truth in the Word.

We are only to pray in Spirit to our GOD the Father and ask of HIM by the NAME of HIS only "begotten Son", so we show HIM that we honor HIS Son, as we also honor HIM, our GOD the Father. Exactly as HE tells us to in the "Testimony of our GOD the Father" concerning HIS Son, our Lord Jesus Christ. We must live by this New Covenant of the Spirit and believe that our Lord Jesus Christ was sent by our GOD the Father from Heaven to Earth for our salvation to have Life, as our GOD the Father said in HIS Testimony about Him, HIS Son.

Everyone that answers the call of our GOD the Father has one thought in their Mind, and that is "I just want to know the Truth". And this is what our Lord Jesus Christ has taught us is the Truth. He prays to and lives in Spirit for our GOD His Father, and we must pray to live in Spirit for our GOD the Father. We all live in Spirit "for" our GOD the Father by obeying HIS command that we must also honor HIS Son. To honor HIS Son we must worship our GOD the Father by acknowledging the NAME of HIS Son Jesus Christ as our Lord. Therefore, we must only pray in Spirit without a doubt to our GOD the Father and by the NAME of our Lord Jesus Christ, HIS only begotten Son.

"We are living in complete unity through our Lord Jesus Christ the Son

Chapter 12: Rejoice in the NAME, Jesus Christ

for our GOD the Father".

- **1 Corinthians 8:6 (NIV)**
  *6 Yet for us there is but One GOD, the Father, "**from**" whom all things came and "**for**" whom we live; and there is but One Lord, Jesus Christ, "**through**" whom all things came and "**through**" whom we live.*

All our blessings and gifts are given to us by our GOD, the Father, and through our Lord Jesus Christ, the Son. When we give thanks to our GOD the Father, we must pray in Spirit **through** our Lord Jesus Christ **to** give thanks to our GOD the Father in good faith.

Some people foolishly think that their god can be whatever they want to believe it is. That is not written for you to do anywhere in the Word of our GOD the Father. That's called having an "idol", which comes from the double minds of the confused, ignorant, and selfish who feel entitled to do and believe whatever they want. They don't really know our GOD the Father or His Son, our Lord Jesus Christ. They say what they imagine can be their god and fool themselves without proof of what they say. Believing in imaginary idols is not true to the Word of our Lord Jesus Christ, who was in the Holy presence of our true living GOD the Father before the World was made. Only He really knows our GOD the Father more than anyone else. And those that believe in Him, our Lord Jesus Christ the Son of our GOD the Father, know the truth about HIM our living GOD the Father of all creation. This is why our Lord Jesus Christ was sent to teach us the Word of Truth about Sin, Judgement, and Life.

This is the Word, and it is the Truth.

The only way to believe the Testimony of our GOD the Father concerning our Lord Jesus Christ is to know THEM first by learning who THEY are. Contemplating the Gospel of our Lord Jesus Christ who teaches us the Word of Truth is the only way to know HIM and then to believe in HIM and our Lord Jesus Christ without a doubt. This is how we build strong faith on a solid foundation that will not fail us. We keep the Word of Truth in our hearts, mind, and soul to have the most powerful faith to do and say what we need to save us from falling away from it.

There is only One True GOD, who is good and HE is the only living Almighty GOD to all HIS creations whether they know it or not. And our Lord Jesus Christ was created in the divinity of GOD, that is in HIS perfect divine image and nature of love, enough to personify the perfect Word and love of our GOD the Father who is love. So perfect that our GOD the Father could dwell in Him and HE was pleased to dwell with HIS fullness in Him.

Just remember, He was created the Son of GOD, not to be confused with our GOD the Father HIMSELF. Therefore, it is written in the Word of Truth that our Lord Jesus Christ was with our GOD the Father at the beginning of creation. He was born first before all creation, and our Lord Jesus Christ made sure that we recognize His position as Servant to our GOD the Father by proclaiming it to others. And it is marked in the message of the written Word of Truth for us to know and honor Him as the Son of the living GOD our Father. We must take the same mindset as Servants to our GOD the Father through our Lord Jesus Christ.

- ### Colossians 1:19-20 (NIV)
    19 For GOD was pleased to have all HIS fullness dwell in Him, 20 and through Him (Jesus Christ) *to reconcile to* (GOD the Father) *HIMSELF all things, whether things on Earth or things in Heaven, by* making peace through (Jesus Christ) His Blood, shed on the cross.

- ### Colossians 1:15 (NIV)
    15 The Son is the image of the invisible GOD, the Firstborn over all creation.

Chapter 12: Rejoice in the NAME, Jesus Christ

- **Philippians 2 (NIV)**

    5 In your relationships with one another, have the same mindset as Christ Jesus: 6 who, being in very nature GOD, did not consider equality with GOD, something to be used to His own advantage; 7 rather, He made Himself nothing by taking the very nature of a Servant, being made in Human Likeness.

Therefore, our Lord Jesus Christ refers to our GOD the Father as His own Father, which means His "Creator". That is why our Lord Jesus Christ said, "No one is good, except GOD alone."

- **Mark 10:17-18 (NIV)**

    17 As Jesus started on His way, a man ran up to Him and fell on his knees before Him. "Good Teacher," he asked, "what must I do to inherit eternal Life?" 18 "Why do you call Me good?" Jesus answered. "No one is good—except GOD alone."

Through our Lord Jesus Christ, the created WORD of our GOD the Father, the rest of creation was created, including the Heavens and Earth. Therefore, it was written in the Word of Truth, that the World did not recognize our Lord Jesus Christ, even though they stood on the World that was created through Him, by the will and power of our Almighty GOD the Father.

Our Lord Jesus Christ is the "Chosen One", the first and only begotten Son, who sits in Heaven with our GOD the Father interceding for us, as our Advocate atoning for our sins now if we should sin again and repent for our weakness. And our GOD the Father predestined all things to be created through His first and only begotten Son because He is the "Christ", the "Anointed One", and the "Chosen One" that was glorified in Heaven before the creation of the Earth; and then glorified again in Heaven after He was raised up; raised up from the dead by the Holy Spirit of our GOD the Father and then He immediately returned to our GOD the Father in Heaven. Our GOD the Father gave our Lord Jesus Christ the power of eternal Life in Him and the Authority to give eternal life to whoever believes in Him. Therefore, He is the "WORD of Life".

- **John 1:10-12 (NIV)**
  10 He was in the World, and though the World was made through Him, the World did not recognize Him. (Jesus Christ) *11 He came to that which was His own,* (people) *but His own did not receive Him. 12 Yet to all who did receive Him, to those who believed in His NAME* (Jesus Christ)*, He gave the right to become Children of GOD—*

Keep in mind, our Lord Jesus Christ is our first helper sent by our GOD the Father from Heaven to Teach us the Word of Truth, so we may also teach others how to be reconciled back to our GOD the Father. He is the living WORD, living in our GOD the Father, and our GOD the Father is living in our Lord Jesus Christ together as One in Spirit. And now THEY are living in us as One with our personal Spirit. And with the same unity that THEY have, we now have with THEM in complete unity. And the same Holy Spirit will raise us up from death to eternal Life to be instantly transformed into an imperishable Spirit Body in the Spirit Realm at our appointed time.

It started with THEM since the beginning of creation, and before the beginning of time as we know it, when our Lord Jesus Christ was the first created, the firstborn, the only begotten Son of our GOD the Father. And all things created after our Lord Jesus Christ were created through Him by the power of our GOD the Father, in which all things are possible. And so, the Apostle John wrote:

Chapter 12: Rejoice in the NAME, Jesus Christ

- **1 John 1:1-4 (NIV)**

    1 That which was from the beginning, (Jesus Christ) which we have HEARD, which we have SEEN with our eyes, which we have LOOKED at and our hands have TOUCHED—this we proclaim concerning the "WORD of Life." (Jesus Christ) 2 The "Life" appeared; (Jesus Christ) we have seen it and Testified to it, and we proclaim to you the "eternal Life", (Jesus Christ) which was with the Father and has appeared to us. 3 We proclaim to you what we have seen and heard, so that you also may have fellowship with us. And our fellowship is with the Father and with HIS Son, Jesus Christ. 4 We write this to make our joy complete.

At the Last Hour with our Lord Jesus Christ, the Apostles did not yet have the Holy Spirit sent from GOD the Father to help them understand everything they were being taught before our Lord Jesus Christ returned to our GOD the Father. So, they could not bear to be told too much more at that time. And now, since our Lord Jesus Christ did return and sits at the Right Hand of our GOD the Father in Heaven, the Apostles and disciples of our Lord Jesus Christ are now sent another Helper, the Holy Spirit that comes out from our GOD the Father to live in us forever.

The Holy Spirit helps us understand what our GOD the Father is doing for each of us at any moment in our lives. The Holy Spirit is the Second Helper sent to guide us and teach us in all the Word of Truth so we may live exceptionally now, as Holy Children of our GOD the Father and Co-Heirs with our Lord Jesus Christ now and later after our redemption on the Last Day when we are taken up by our Lord Jesus Christ to live with THEM. We are wise to learn and accept living by the Word of Truth in the Spirit. And those that do not are foolish.

- **Mathew 7: N.I.V.**

    24 "Therefore everyone who hears these Words of Mine and puts

> *them into practice is like a wise man who built his house on the rock.* (strong faith) ... **26** *But everyone who hears these Words of Mine and does not put them into practice is like a foolish man who built his house on sand.* ~ (no faith)

When we pay attention, we will hear when He (Jesus Christ) speaks to us through the Holy Spirit. He will tell us and warn us what is about to happen in our lives through our senses, feelings, thoughts, dreams, and Groans from our Hearts by the Holy Spirit. Being told in advance is how we are protected so we can take corrective action or prepare to stay safe ourselves and help others learn to do the same. And when that happens, our Lord Jesus Christ will be glorified by the Holy Spirit because that is what He said would happen by the Holy Spirit. When you let the Holy Spirit guide you throughout your Life, that is a blessing by our GOD the Father. It is truly a miracle happening in you. Because HIS Holy Spirit is living as One with you in your heart and interceding for you to our GOD the Father to help you.

Our GOD the Father knows you and understands exactly where you are in your Life, and more importantly, HE loves you more than you can believe, and HE will prove it to you. Move closer to HIM and HE will move closer to you. From now on remember, you are living as a "Spirit Person" living in our Lord Jesus Christ, with Him living in you. Since He lives, you live; and since He has eternal Life in Himself, you have eternal Life in yourself. You must thank our GOD the Father through our Lord Jesus Christ, for that. Through the Holy Spirit, we have a Spirit relationship with our Lord Jesus Christ. He tells the Holy Spirit what to tell us for our own good. We are never alone without the help of our GOD the Father in our Lord Jesus Christ, and with the Holy Spirit living in us with our own personal Spirit that we were born within our Body-Temple.

Our personal Spirit is that which we were created into in Heaven, by our GOD the Father. At the beginning of living our life, our Spirit was formed with the flesh from our biological Mother. When your Spirit

Chapter 12: Rejoice in the NAME, Jesus Christ

leaves the body, the body dies, and your personal Spirit will wait in sleep for the Voice of our Lord Jesus Christ that will call you up to the Heavens and raise you up by the Holy Spirit for eternal Life. As a purified Spirit Child belonging to our GOD the Father, no one can condemn your personal Spirit. Only by the authority of our GOD the Father can your personal Spirit ever be condemned and finally executed. And our Lord Jesus Christ has been given the Authority of Judgement above all creation in Heaven, Earth, and Under Earth.

With Him living in unity with you now, you have no sin in you now to be judged by. Because, you have already been forgiven for all your sins by our Lord Jesus Christ living in you, and you have crossed over from death to Life within Him. You are living a Holy Life as a Holy Child of our GOD the Father now. And no harm of evil can ever harm your personal Spirit with the Holy Spirit and our Lord Jesus Christ living in you and with our GOD the Father living in Him.

- 1 John 5:18-20 (NIV)

    18 We know that anyone Born of GOD does not continue to sin; the One (Jesus Christ) who was Born of GOD keeps them safe, and the evil one cannot harm them. 19 We know that we are Children of GOD, and that the whole World is under the control of the evil one. 20 We know also that the Son of GOD has come and has given us understanding, so that we may know HIM (GOD the Father) who is True. And we are in Him (GOD the Father) who is True, by being in HIS Son Jesus Christ. HE (GOD the Father) is the True GOD and eternal Life.

Remember, Satan now stands condemned. That is his "status", and the status of anyone who does not have our Lord Jesus Christ living in them; that is judgment. Along with Satan, those who do not have a Spirit relationship with our Lord Jesus Christ are also condemned now and doomed to destruction at their appointed time for not accepting Him. That is their final execution for their condemnation. Our Lord Jesus Christ said that the Holy Spirit will teach us and prove the World wrong about Sin, Righteousness, and Judgement.

-**About Sin**, because our Lord Jesus Christ said that He will speak to us through the Holy Spirit and that is how He will show Himself to believers in Him. When the Holy Spirit comes to you and you know He is proving Himself to you, then that proves everything that our Lord Jesus Christ said is true, that Satan corrupts the whole World with his ways of sin. We must reject Satan by rejecting his sinful ways of living. And how not believing in our Lord Jesus Christ is a sin. It's as bad as calling Him a liar about the things He said, that the works He performed were being done through Him by our GOD the Father, and that He was sent by our GOD the Father from Heaven to us on Earth for our salvation. We must believe the Truth in the Word in our hearts and live by the Testimony of our GOD the Father to have eternal Life without sin now.

-**About Righteousness**, because our Lord Jesus Christ returned to Heaven and sits at the Right Hand of our GOD the Father atoning for our sins that we repent, therefore, since He destroyed the power of sin in the flesh by not sinning, our Lord Jesus Christ defeated sin with His Righteousness, which proves that Righteousness is more powerful than sin. By having the Righteous Requirement of our Lord Jesus Christ in us, we overcome sin with the power of His Righteousness.

The Righteousness in our Lord Jesus Christ prevails over sin because our Lord Jesus Christ has kept the commands of our GOD the Father and suffered to death without sin, to destroy sin in the flesh and bring the fulfillment of the Righteous Requirement into our souls living in the Spirit, making us Holy in complete unity with THEM. And His love for us did overcome the power of sin, so that He may remove it from us now if we believe in Him by keeping His commands to Always Love Each Other.

He was the first to be raised up from the dead and has returned to our GOD the Father in Heaven. He deserves to be glorified forever as He sits at the Right Hand of our GOD the Father in Heaven, atoning for our

Chapter 12: Rejoice in the NAME, Jesus Christ

sins to fulfill us to His Righteous Requirement, by the New Covenant of the Spirit that He is, living in us now. And we now know why the Old Covenant could never fulfill our Righteous Requirement for eternal Life. Only by living in complete unity with our Lord Jesus Christ can our Righteous Requirement to enter eternal Life be met to make us Holy Children of our GOD the Father.

-About Judgement, because no one has the right or the power to condemn another person except by the Authority of our GOD the Father; and only the Son of GOD, our Lord Jesus Christ has been given the Authority to Judge, condemn, and execute since He proved to be completely Righteous by never accepting to sin Himself. And since Satan has sinned in himself as prince of this World, then every one of the World has sinned and is condemned the way the demons are condemned. Our Lord Jesus Christ defeated sin by His Righteousness and is with our GOD the Father now, therefore, Satan and every one of the World stands condemned now with Satan by their own decision to continue to live with sin. And by that, they are going to be destroyed by the power in the Authority of our Lord Jesus Christ to administer the Judgement and destroy all the condemned with their sin. And those who decide to believe in our Lord Jesus Christ by following His commands will not be Judged because they repented their sin and have been forgiven for their sin and they do not sin anymore by being united with our Lord Jesus Christ as One in Spirit.

Judgment for the condemned non-believers will finally be executed by our Lord Jesus Christ in Heaven by His Authority to Judge sinners and execute the Judgement on them for their own status of condemnation for not accepting to believe in the Testimony of our GOD the Father. And at this time, Satan now stands condemned is Judgement awaiting the Final execution to be carried out on the Last Day, the Judgement Day. It will be like the Last Day when the Angels of our GOD the Father Sealed the door to the Ark that Noah built by the command of our GOD the Father. Those who refused to accept the Testimony of our GOD the Father and believe in HIM were destroyed by their decision after being warned for

120 years to turn from their sinful ways.

Now is your appointed time to Decide to accept or reject the New Covenant of our GOD the Father before the door is closed on you and you live your last day on Earth. The whole World is condemned by sin and is being warned. And each of us must Decide to stay condemned or accept the Choice of our GOD the Father to enter eternal Life through having HIS Son, our Lord Jesus Christ in complete unity. This is the appointed time of the New Covenant.

All those who believe in our Lord Jesus Christ are saved from the Judgement for sin because the sin in them has been forgiven and removed from them by the power and Righteousness of our Lord Jesus Christ living in them, giving them eternal Life. He told the Apostles: "Because I live, you will live." now you know why He said that. If you believe without a doubt, in our Lord Jesus Christ, and believe with all your Heart, your Soul, and your Mind, that He was sent to us from our GOD the Father; then pray in Spirit to our GOD the Father to submit and commit yourself to HIM and ask HIM to send HIS Holy Spirit into you in the NAME of our Lord Jesus Christ HIS Son. Then learn the Word and listen to the Holy Spirit guide you to keep you living by the Word.

Do it now, if you haven't already asked, because by reading and hearing the Word in these Chapters, you are now sanctified by the Truth that you know. You know the Truth, that the will of our GOD the Father is for everyone to have eternal Life, and that Life is in HIS Son, if you have the Son of GOD, you have Life. HIS Choice is for us to accept to believe in HIM and HIS Son to have a Life that will last. You are forgiven for all your sins if you just believe in HIM without doubt and repent your sins to our GOD the Father in the NAME of HIS Son, our Lord Jesus Christ.

You may now be given the Right to live as a Holy Child of our GOD the Father through HIS Son, our Lord Jesus Christ. Remember, no one can enter eternal Life without believing in the Testimony of our GOD the Father.

Chapter 12: Rejoice in the NAME, Jesus Christ

This is the Word of our GOD the Father, and it is the Truth.

- **1 John 5:11-12 (NIV)**
  11 And this is the Testimony: ***GOD has given us eternal Life, and this Life is in HIS Son. 12 Whoever has the Son has Life;*** *whoever does not have the Son of GOD does not have Life.*

With the Holy Spirit as a promise in you to redeem you to enter eternal Life in the Kingdom of Heaven because you now have salvation from death and sin by the innocent Blood Sacrifice that was shed on the cross by our Lord Jesus Christ for your weakness in sin. And by having our Lord Jesus Christ in you now, you now have eternal Life, because our Lord Jesus Christ in you has eternal Life in Him. He is eternal Life with our GOD the Father who is eternal Life, and He is the WORD of Life with our GOD the Father dwelling in Him that gives us all eternal Life.

This is the Word, and it is the Truth.

Believe without a doubt, that you now belong to our GOD the Father through our Lord Jesus Christ. And that you are alive and living in Spirit with the Holy Spirit for eternal Life in complete unity.

AND THIS IS OUR PRAYER:

We pray in Spirit to You, our GOD the Father in Heaven, for sending Your Son, our Lord Jesus Christ, to teach us Your Word of Truth and to save us out of this World with the eternal Life that You put in Him. May Your Holy Spirit guide us to keep Your commands in the Word from Your Son, our Lord Jesus Christ. We thank You for Your protection from any evil one, by the power in the NAME of our Lord Jesus Christ.

We pray to ask You in the NAME of our Lord Jesus Christ.

INSPIRATION FOR YOUR ETERNAL LIFE

Chapter 12: *Rejoice in the NAME, Jesus Christ*

John 16:16-27 NIV

16 "Jesus went on to say, "In a little while you will see Me no more, and then after a little while you will see Me."

17 At this, some of His Disciples said to one another, "What does He mean by saying, 'In a little while you will see Me no more, and then after a little while you will see Me,' and Because I am going to the Father?"

18 They kept asking, "What does He mean by 'a little while'? We don't understand what He is saying."

19 Jesus saw that they wanted to ask Him about this, so He said to them, "Are you asking one another what I meant when I said, 'In a little while you will see Me no more, and then after a little while you will see Me?

20 Very truly I tell you, you will weep and mourn while the World rejoices. You will grieve, but your grief will turn to joy.

21 A woman giving birth to a child has pain because her time has come; but when her baby is born she forgets the anguish because of her joy that a child is born into the World.

22 So with you: Now is your time of grief, but I will see you again and you will rejoice, and no one will take away your joy.

23 In that day you will no longer ask Me anything. **Very truly I tell you**, My Father will give you whatever you ask in My NAME.

Chapter 12: Rejoice in the NAME, Jesus Christ

<u>24</u> Until now you have not asked for anything in My NAME. Ask and you will receive, and your joy will be complete.

<u>25</u> "Though I have been speaking figuratively, a time is coming when I will no longer use this kind of language but will tell you plainly about My Father.

<u>26</u> In that day you will ask in My NAME. I am not saying that I will ask the Father on your behalf.

27 No, the Father HIMSELF loves you because you have loved Me and have believed that I came from GOD.

❖ Notice:

Our Lord Jesus Christ was talking about what will happen after His resurrection and His return to the Apostles in a little while. And one reason why He went back to our GOD the Father is to ask HIM to send HIS Holy Spirit to the Apostles and all believers in Him. Until the commands of our GOD the Father for Him were all completed, and He returned and asked of our GOD the Father, HIS Holy Spirit would not be sent into anyone from our GOD the Father by our Lord Jesus Christ. Our Lord Jesus Christ was letting them know who He is and how the Apostles could trust in Him and believe in Him about the Testimony of our GOD the Father. That is why our Lord Jesus Christ teaches that if you believe in our GOD the Father, believe also in HIS Son Jesus Christ.

This is exactly what our GOD the Father wants us to know concerning His only begotten Son Jesus Christ; that we must honor HIS Son by asking of HIM by praying in Spirit in the NAME of HIS Son Jesus Christ to prove that we believe without a doubt in HIS Son Jesus Christ and that HE HIMSELF our GOD the Father proves that HE loves us enough to make HIS New Covenant with us by HIS own will. HIS New Covenant gives us more Grace with the GIFT of HIS glory that is of HIS eternal Life that comes from within HIM. HE glorified HIS Son, our

Lord Jesus Christ with this power of eternal Life in Him when He fulfilled all HIS commands and prophesies of the Old Covenant that was made transitory; and by the Righteousness in the Sacrificial Sacred Blood Shed and Death of our Lord Jesus Christ, the Old Covenant has been Transcended and has passed away, which makes it's ineffectiveness to fulfill us with the righteous requirement to have eternal Life to be overshadowed by the New Covenant. Since then, the New Covenant of the Spirit now brings into effect the Spirit of our Lord Jesus Christ that gives His eternal Life to us by having Him in complete unity with our personal Spirit to include the Holy Spirit of our GOD the Father forever.

By HIS mercy on our lowly beings, His Word will be carried out by HIS glory of eternal Life that HE glorified HIS Son with, to give this Life to anyone that believes in THEM and accepts our Lord Jesus Christ into their Heart, to bring His eternal Life into us with His Spirit and the Holy Spirit from our GOD the Father, for us to live in complete unity with THEM as One with our personal Spirit in our Body-Temple, which makes us Children of GOD. This is how through our Lord Jesus Christ our GOD the Father has taken us to a HIGHER GRACE that we may be transformed into imperishable Spirit Beings to become Children of GOD by HIS Son our Lord Jesus Christ. Therefore, our Lord Jesus Christ let us know that no one will see our GOD the Father to have eternal Life except through believing in and accepting our Lord Jesus Christ as our Lord, Teacher, and Savior who has this Life in Himself to give and glorify all His Disciples with.

As it is for us to believe in our Lord Jesus Christ to have Life, until the Apostles believed in Him without a doubt to be completely sanctified, they would not be ready to receive His Spirit or the Holy Spirit of our GOD the Father in themselves for His eternal Life. That is why our Lord Jesus Christ continued to prophesy until His chosen ones were certain that He is the Son of our GOD the Father and was sent by HIM for our salvation to transform us to a Higher Grace to live with THEM as Holy Children of our GOD the Father now and later after our transformation into an imperishable Spirit Body in the Heavens.

Chapter 12: Rejoice in the NAME, Jesus Christ

This is the Word, and it is the Truth.

This foretold event also proves to the World that our Lord Jesus Christ was sent from Heaven by our GOD the Father because they did see Him alive again. And with eternal Life in Him, as the Word of Life, they did see Him again after His resurrection by the Holy Spirit of our GOD the Father, because He said He will show Himself to those who believe in Him. Their faith in Him was complete and their hope with joy was fulfilled when our Lord Jesus Christ appeared to them as He said He would to be the witnesses of His resurrection so they may teach the World about Him and our GOD the Father firsthand and write scriptures for us to believe them by that which is the Gospel of our Lord Jesus Christ in the New TESTAMENT. And all those who believe in Him by faith in the Gospel do not need to see Him with their eyes because He proves Himself by His works from within each person and by His Spirit living in each person without a doubt.

By then, our GOD the Father sent HIS Holy Spirit into them to guide, teach, comfort, and intercede from within them to our GOD the Father, by knowing what their heart desires and need to ask, so they would never need to question our Lord Jesus Christ ever again. We will only need to ask of our GOD the Father in the NAME of HIS Son Jesus Christ on our own behalf because our GOD the Father loves us. Our GOD the Father provided for them whatever they needed to have to glorify our GOD the Father in the same way He did for our Lord Jesus Christ on Earth.

We have the Holy Spirit of our GOD the Father telling and showing us what our Lord Jesus Christ wants us to know to keep us safe in our life now. It is from Him that the Holy Spirit gets what to tell and show us. Therefore, we will do everything in word or deed giving thanks to our GOD the Father in the NAME of our Lord Jesus Christ. When it is your time to glorify our GOD the Father, HIS Holy Spirit will compel your heart to do what HE wants you to do or say to glorify HIM. That is how we are guided in Spirit by HIS Holy Spirit. Praise be to our GOD the Father in the NAME of HIS Son, our Lord Jesus Christ.

We can feel the power of the Holy Spirit working in our hearts and teaching us with the love our Lord Jesus Christ wants us to have. That is how we know we are living in complete unity with THEM in us, we feel it in our heart where our Spirit speaks from. When we feel love or other emotions, we feel it in our heart first then we figure out what it means and what to do in accordance with our feelings. And the Holy Spirit will let you know from your heart what you are about to do or are doing is good or bad. That is why we must submit ourselves completely with our Heart, Mind, and Soul, to our GOD the Father in Spirit prayer that our personal Spirit speaks from our Heart.

If you are thinking and speaking from your heart in Spirit prayer to our GOD the Father, in the NAME of HIS Son Jesus Christ our Lord, then the Holy Spirit of our GOD the Father will interpret exactly what you mean without you saying a word from your mouth out loud. Therefore, whatever you do or say, do it all giving thanks to our GOD the Father and in the NAME of HIS Son to give honor to THEM both, and HIS Holy Spirit will help you pray what you mean, even if you can't find the words, He knows what you mean to say and He will say it for you to our GOD the Father in accordance to HIS will for you as HIS Child.

You are never left alone living in complete unity knowing THEY are with you forever. Then our Lord Jesus Christ gives glory to our GOD the Father by telling us, He is not going to ask our GOD the Father for you, on your behalf. Because our GOD the Father loves us for believing that HE sent HIS Son, and HE knows we love HIS Son as our Lord Jesus Christ when we give thanks to our GOD the Father in the NAME of HIS Son our Lord Jesus Christ. That is honoring our GOD the Father through honoring HIS Son our Lord Jesus Christ by praying in Spirit, exactly as our Lord Jesus Christ teaches us how to pray to glorify our GOD the Father and accept HIS Word with HIS Testimony. We also show we believe in Him when we practice living by the Word, He Teaches us to keep His New command to Love One Another. Practice living by the Word makes your Spirit Holy and perfect with the guidance of the Holy Spirit received from our Lord Jesus Christ.

Chapter 12: Rejoice in the NAME, Jesus Christ

Remember, we are the Branches bearing fruit for eternal Life remaining attached to the Vine, our Lord Jesus Christ. Without His helping us we will not have Life and without helping others learn the Word of Truth we will be cut off by our GOD the Father from the Life in Him. That is why, as the Apostles and the Disciples of our Lord Jesus Christ, we can ask of our GOD the Father ourselves in the NAME of our Lord Jesus Christ for anything we need to glorify our GOD the Father and HE will hear our prayer first to save us out from condemnation so we may cross over from death into Life in our Body-Temple now. Our Lord Jesus Christ will also help us from within us in complete unity. We are made Holy with THEM dwelling with our personal Spirit in our Holy Body-Temple. Strive to stay Holy and worthy of the Gospel about our Lord Jesus Christ.

If you believe in our Lord Jesus Christ, then you are His disciples by learning and following His commands in the Word while living in the Spirit with Him. And that is living with His Spirit of eternal Life and living with the Holy Spirit of our GOD the Father in your Body-Temple now. You are His disciples living in complete unity in Spirit with our Lord Jesus Christ. Our GOD the Father is in unity within our Lord Jesus Christ, therefore only through Him and by accepting having Him in us now, will we see our GOD the Father in Heaven and enter into eternal Life in HIS Kingdom. Keep living to please the Holy Spirit while He is living in complete unity in you. And stay focused on Heavenly things, not Worldly things, so that our GOD the Father may bless you and your family now and for the Last Day, the Lord's Day, when we are all miraculously transformed into Spirit Bodies to meet our Lord Jesus Christ in the clouds with our Holy loved ones.

This is the Word, and it is the Truth.

- **Philippians 3:20-21 (NIV)**
  [20] But our Citizenship is in Heaven, and we eagerly await a Savior from there, the Lord Jesus Christ, [21] who, by the power that enables Him to bring everything under His

control, will transform our lowly Bodies so that they will be like His glorious Body.

At the beginning of humanity in the flesh and before "the Word", who is our Lord Jesus Christ, was sent to Earth by our GOD the Father and created Him into flesh and Spirit, believers in our GOD the Father would pray to ask of HIM directly. Our Lord Jesus Christ was not sent here to change that. He was sent here to support that and help us understand the Truth as our Teacher, Lord, and Savior; and to support that we ourselves can ask of our GOD the Father by Praying in Spirit, to be reconciled back to HIM in peace. Only now, we are to ask in the NAME of our Lord Jesus Christ to honor Him as the Son of GOD, as we honor our GOD the Father by giving thanks to HIM for sending HIS Son to forgive us for our sins to make us righteous in the presence of our GOD the Father for eternal Life. Because our GOD the Father sent Him for us to believe in Him and follow Him as our Teacher, Lord, and Savior for our salvation from sin and death to have eternal Life. We must accept Him into our hearts, so we may have His eternal Life living in us. Remember, no one can enter into eternal Life without believing in the Testimony of our GOD the Father.

- 1 John 5:11-12 (NIV)
    11 And this is the Testimony: **GOD has given us eternal Life, and this Life is in HIS Son.** *12* **Whoever has the Son has Life; whoever does not have the Son of GOD does not have Life.**

- John 17:3-4 (NIV)
    3 Now this is eternal Life: that they know You, (GOD the Father) *the only True GOD, and* (HIS Son) *Jesus Christ, whom You* (GOD the Father) *have sent. 4 I have brought*

Chapter 12: Rejoice in the NAME, Jesus Christ

you glory on Earth by finishing the work You gave Me to do.

At the time we Decide to believe in our Lord Jesus Christ and accept Him to be in "complete unity" in us, we cross over from death in the flesh, to eternal Life in the Spirit with THEM in us. We do this by repenting our sin first, then praying in Spirit to receive the Holy Spirit into us from our GOD the Father, in the NAME of HIS Son, our Lord Jesus Christ. Receiving the Holy Spirit in the NAME of our Lord Jesus Christ is being Baptized when we receive into us the "Holy Spirit and Fire".

That is how John The Baptist described how Baptism would be in the NAME of our Lord Jesus Christ. This is also referred to as you are "Reborn", "Blessed", "Filled, or "Anointed" with the Holy Spirit of our GOD the Father in the NAME of our Lord Jesus Christ. It is Truly a miracle to receive HIS Holy Spirit to be living in you and helping you on a daily basis, proving that our Lord Jesus Christ loves us in many ways and is living within us in Spirit.

This is the Word, and it is the Truth.

- ### Acts 2:38-39, 41 (NIV)
    38 Peter replied, "Repent and be baptized, every one of you, in the NAME of Jesus Christ for the forgiveness of your sins. And you will receive the Gift of the Holy Spirit. (eternal Life)
    39 The Promise is for you and your children and for all who are far off— For all whom the LORD our GOD will call." (GOD the Father)

    41 Those who accepted his message were baptized, and about Three Thousand added to their number that day.

And it will be done at the time you believe the Testimony of our GOD the Father because that is what our Lord Jesus Christ said will be done. And at that time, you are given the right to become a Holy Child of our GOD the Father by having our Lord Jesus Christ forgiving you and making you Holy and Co-Heir with our Lord Jesus Christ to the New Kingdom because you now belong to our GOD the Father. And THEY will care for you more by being within you forever from that time forward. This is part of HIS Designed Grand Plan to reconcile all Creation in Heaven and Earth back to our GOD the Father HIMSELF. And HE will live among us in HIS created New World Kingdom. The Kingdom is our future Home with HIM.

Our Lord Jesus Christ is not our messenger to relay whatever we want to ask of our GOD the Father. We must worship our GOD the Father and ask of HIM on our own behalf for ourselves while living and praying in the Spirit. The same way our Lord Jesus Christ did pray to our GOD the Father in Heaven when He, our Lord Jesus Christ was on Earth. Because our GOD the Father is Spirit and looks for those that worship HIM in the Spirit. Our Lord Jesus Christ is the living Word of Life and the example of what we ourselves should say and do. His will is for us to live in His Nature now and become like His image.

Our GOD the Father gave us a New Covenant to have eternal Life. We must Decide to accept the Choice HE made for us with HIS mercy to give us eternal Life in HIS Son Jesus Christ by accepting to have Him living within us in complete unity. Let your Spirit shine from your heart like a lighthouse beacon for everyone lost in the sea of corruption to find their way to eternal Life in our Lord Jesus Christ as they are being called by our GOD the Father to gather them unto HIMSELF. The Message is written in our hearts and we must help others by sharing with them our gifts and our Testimony of what our Lord Jesus Christ has done for us over time. And anyone that turns to Him for Life will not be turned away.

Chapter 12: Rejoice in the NAME, Jesus Christ

This is the Word, and it is the Truth of our GOD the Father.

- ## 2 Corinthians 3:2-18 (NIV)

    2 You yourselves are our Letter, written on our Hearts, known and read by everyone. 3 You show that you are a Letter from Christ, the result of our Ministry, written not with ink but with the Spirit of the LIVING GOD, not on tablets of stone but on tablets of human hearts. 4 Such confidence we have through Christ before GOD. 5 Not that we are competent in ourselves to claim anything for ourselves, but our competence comes from GOD. 6 HE has made us competent as Ministers of a New Covenant—not of the letter but of the Spirit; for the letter kills (Old Covenant), but the Spirit gives (New Covenant) 7 Now if the Ministry that brought death, which was engraved in letters on stone, (Old Covenant) came with glory, so that the Israelites could not look steadily at the face of Moses because of its glory, transitory though it was, 8 will not the Ministry of the Spirit be even more glorious? (New Covenant) 9 If the Ministry that brought condemnation was glorious, (The Old Covenant) how much more glorious is the Ministry that brings righteousness! (The New Covenant) 10 For what was glorious has no glory now (Old Covenant) in comparison with the Surpassing glory. (New Covenant) 11 And if what was transitory came with glory (Old Covenant), how much greater is the glory of that which lasts! (New Covenant) 12 Therefore, since we have such a hope, we are very bold. 13 We are not like Moses, who would put a veil over his face to prevent the Israelites from seeing the end of what was passing away. (Old Covenant) 14 But their minds were made dull, for to this day the same veil remains when the Old Covenant is read. It has not been removed, Because only in Christ is it taken away. (New Covenant) 15 Even to this day when Moses is read, a veil covers their hearts. (Old Covenant) 16 But whenever anyone turns to the Lord, the veil is taken away.

(New Covenant) *17 Now the Lord is the Spirit, and where the Spirit of the Lord is, there is freedom. 18 And we all, who with unveiled faces contemplate the Lord's glory, are being transformed into His image with ever-increasing glory, which comes from the Lord, who is the Spirit. ~* (New Covenant)

Now you know why we have a New Command, in the New Covenant, written in the New Testament. What the Old Covenant could not do, our GOD the Father did by HIS New Covenant for us through our Lord Jesus Christ, in that HE gives us eternal Life for all that believe in HIS Truth, in HIS Word, and in HIS own Testimony of our GOD the Father. It is not even to our credit that we have this Choice because it was made for us without us doing anything to make it happen. Because it isn't a Choice that we can even make, the Choice is HIS will for us given as a gift. We cannot make anything without the power of our GOD the Father. It is only by the mercy and love that our GOD the Father has for us that HE created this Choice as a gift for us. This Choice is a gift of eternal Life that we can only receive by our Decision to believe in and accept, when we accept to believe in HIS Son, our Lord Jesus Christ, by accepting Him into our hearts to live in complete unity within us.

Every person that exists now on Earth without having our Lord Jesus Christ living in themselves now is standing condemned without Him. We only have a Decision to accept the Choice our GOD the Father has made and given to us. We only need to Decide to believe in THEM, to know THEM by the Testimony of our GOD the Father and accept to live by the New Covenant. And that is a Decision to be led by the Guidance of His Holy Spirit in us for everything we say or do. That includes having the Life of our Lord Jesus Christ living in us in complete unity.

To live in complete unity is to live in the Church, who is our Lord Jesus Christ, and within Him all believers that are now as One in Him. And that is being One with THEM as THEY, our Lord Jesus Christ and our GOD the Father are as One, we are now One with THEM forever. That is the

Chapter 12: Rejoice in the NAME, Jesus Christ

Crossing Over from death to eternal Life living in Spirit, within our Body-Temple now. There is no other Way, or NAME, except by the NAME of our Lord Jesus Christ. He is the only way to eternal Life with our GOD the Father. This is HIS will and the will of our Lord Jesus Christ that they want for us to live eternal Life with THEM in Paradise. Our GOD the Father wants us to ask of HIM in the Holy NAME of HIS Anointed One, "Jesus Christ," so we express to HIM that we keep the Word exactly how our Lord Jesus Christ teaches us to do and ask by our prayers in Spirit to glorify our GOD the Father. This is the kind of worshippers our GOD the Father is looking for, the ones that prove that they believe HIS Testimony.

The Holy NAME of our Lord Jesus Christ was given by our GOD the Father to HIS only begotten Son, who was created and chosen to be the "Anointed One" in Heaven at a Time in the past beyond our imagination. It was before Time began as we know it on Earth because it was before the Earth was created. He was the first created meaning: the first- Born of all Creation. And He was glorified as the Christ meaning: the Anointed One and Chosen One. He is the Chosen One by our GOD the Father to be our Savior to reconcile us back to HIMSELF. The NAME of our Lord Jesus Christ certainly was given to Him before the creation of the Earth by our GOD the Father.

That is why our GOD the Father sent the Angel Gabriel, HIS messenger from Heaven to reveal to Mary that she will conceive and NAME her baby "Jesus". Because that NAME with its meaning and created power has a purpose that was already given by our GOD the Father at the time our Lord Jesus Christ was the first created or she would not have been told to NAME Him Jesus. If that were not true, our Lord Jesus Christ would not have asked for our protection by the NAME He was given before the World was created.

This translation is written in our English Language to refer to our Lord Jesus Christ. And our GOD the Father searches our Heart as HE hears the Wordless Groans HIS Holy Spirit tells HIM exactly what and who we are calling on, in any language before we speak. And HE will answer your calling even if you can't speak because the Holy Spirit in you speaks for you from your Heart to our GOD the Father in Wordless Groans that our GOD the Father understands. Your heart cries out and is understood and interpreted by the Holy Spirit before your Mind knows what to say. Anything you feel in your Heart is felt by the Holy Spirit, who is constantly finding ways to help you throughout your spiritual Life in complete unity with our Lord Jesus Christ in you.

That is why we feel what we desire in our hearts first before we figure out what it means. And we feel the love in our Heart so strong to be One with our GOD the Father and with our Lord Jesus Christ; and before we can think it or say yes, we already said it in our heart. Our GOD the Father hears you by HIS Holy Spirit living in you because you live and pray in the Spirit to HIM in the NAME of HIS Son Jesus Christ. We are always being tested for our faith to become stronger in faith. So, be careful of impure thoughts that may come to your Mind that may lead to sin. Purge them with the Word of Truth that you know in the NAME of our Lord Jesus Christ that will save your life and keep you away from sin.

If you haven't already, and you believe in Him without a doubt, then pray in Spirit now to our GOD the Father in the NAME of our Lord Jesus Christ for yourself to accept the Holy Spirit in you. Then our Lord Jesus Christ, with the power Vested in Him by our GOD the Father, will do it for you. He will not turn you away.

- **John 17:5 (NIV)**

    5 And now, Father, glorify Me (Jesus Christ) in Your presence with the glory I had with You before the World began.

- **John 17:11-12 (NIV)**

Chapter 12: Rejoice in the NAME, Jesus Christ

> *11 .... Holy Father, protect them by the power of Your NAME, the NAME You gave Me* (Jesus Christ), *so that they may be One as WE are One. 12 While I was with them, I protected them and kept them safe by that NAME You gave Me* (Jesus Christ). *None has been lost except* (Judas Iscariot) *the one doomed to destruction so that the Scripture would be fulfilled.*

- ## John 17:24 (NIV)
  > *24 "Father, I want those you have given Me to be with Me where I am* (in Heaven), *and to see My glory, the glory You have given Me because You loved Me before the creation of the World.*

- ## COLOSSIANS 3:17 (NIV)
  > *17 "And whatever you do, whether in word or deed, do it all in the NAME of the Lord Jesus Christ, giving thanks to GOD the Father through Him."*

- **Now we will know the Way to Pray.**

- **Whom we may ask: Our GOD the Father.**

- **When to ask: When praying in Spirit to our GOD the Father and giving thanks for word or deed.**

- **How to ask: Pray in the Spirit to our GOD the Father through our Lord Jesus Christ, in HIS Sons NAME, Jesus Christ.**

We get stronger in faith by learning the Word of Truth, to be sanctified by our GOD the Father in the NAME of our Lord Jesus Christ every day.

What we learn from our Lord Jesus Christ in the Word of Truth, is our instruction on how to live our lives in the Spirit with Him now and for eternal Life. The same way our Lord Jesus Christ is now living in the Spirit.

It doesn't matter what was required by any others in any past covenant for them to be in the good grace of our GOD the Father. In this day and age, our GOD the Father gave us eternal Life in His New Covenant, by sending us HIS Son Jesus Christ to be living in unity within us in Spirit, for us to be reconciled back to our GOD the Father HIMSELF. HIS written Word is given for us to live by in this time period. From the time our Lord Jesus Christ was sent from Heaven and was resurrected from death on the cross, until the time we are redeemed and raised up to enter eternal Life in HIS New World Kingdom. This is where we are today. The Holy Spirit is always our witness in fellowship with our Spirit in us.

Praise be to our GOD the Father. We will be called and raised up, by our Lord Jesus Christ, to be miraculously transformed to live in immortal and imperishable Spirit Bodies in the New Kingdom, on a New Earth, conjoined with a New Heaven with our GOD the Father and our Lord Jesus Christ.

This is the Word, and it is the Truth.

Chapter 12: Rejoice in the NAME, Jesus Christ

<u>*And This Is Our Prayer:*</u>

We pray to give thanks to You, our GOD the Father, as we rejoice in the NAME of our Lord Jesus Christ from our Hearts to You for sending Him to us and giving us the same love that You give to Your Son, our Lord Jesus Christ.

May Your Holy Spirit guide us with your Word of Truth and protect us by the power in the name of our Lord Jesus Christ that we acknowledge in prayer and before others.

We pray in Spirit to ask of You in the NAME of our Lord Jesus Christ.

Chapter 13: Take Heart, our Lord Jesus Christ Rules, Satan Stands Condemned

John 16:28-33 NIV

<u>28</u> I (Jesus Christ) came from the Father and entered the World; Now I am leaving the World and going back to the Father.

<u>29</u> Then Jesus' disciples said, "Now You are speaking clearly and without figures of speech.

<u>30</u> Now we can see that "**You know all things**" and that You do not even need to have anyone ask You questions. "**This makes us believe that You came from GOD.**"

<u>31</u> "Do you now believe?" Jesus replied.

<u>32</u> "A time is coming and in fact has come when you will be scattered, each to your own home. You will leave Me all alone. Yet I am not alone, for My Father is with Me.

<u>33</u> "I have told you these things, so that in Me you may have peace. In this World you will have trouble. But Take heart! **I have Overcome the World.**"

❖ **Notice:**

During their time and travels with our Lord Jesus Christ, the Apostles witnessed the power of our GOD the Father in every miracle He

Chapter 14: Eternal Life is our God the Father and our Lord Jesus Christ

performed through our Lord Jesus Christ, while also hearing what our GOD the Father spoke through our Lord Jesus Christ. Exactly what our Lord Jesus Christ said that our GOD the Father did through Him. And it was just before our Lord Jesus Christ was to be taken and be put to death, that for the very first time the disciples agreed and said,

—

"This makes us believe that You came from GOD".

—

When the disciples honestly believed that He was sent by our GOD the Father, they all believed the Testimony of our GOD the Father had given about our Lord Jesus Christ with certainty. That is the New Covenant for Mankind to believe and obey to reconcile with our GOD the Father. Every believer must believe the Testimony given by our GOD the Father about our Lord Jesus Christ, HIS only begotten Son. The disciples then said that no one needs to question our Lord Jesus Christ, as they had done to test His knowledge of all things, that only the One that was sent from our GOD the Father would know to say and do. They certainly believed that He knew all things. When they admitted those words for the first time, our Lord Jesus Christ had finally saved them, as He obeyed the commands that He was given and sent to do by our GOD the Father in Heaven.

Therefore, after all accounts of questions, answers, time living with Him, hearing Him, seeing Him, and witnessing the Works of Miracles performed through Him, it has been determined by the Apostles in a unanimous belief and Decision that our Lord Jesus Christ is the only begotten Son and did come from our GOD the Father in Heaven. And no one else ever needs to question His Authority or Word of Truth ever again. They witnessed Him, and they believe in Him without any doubt that He is who He said He is, the Son of our GOD the Father.

If anyone doesn't believe that our GOD the Father sent our Lord Jesus Christ, then they are making our GOD the Father out to be a liar. Not only because they don't say they believe the Testimony of our GOD the Father is true, but because they don't show themselves to others that they believe it's true by what they say and do. It is the same as denying that you believe in Him if you do not acknowledge Him before others as your Lord and Savior. Our Lord Jesus Christ will not dwell in those non-believers because they live in fear that they will lose what they have in this World and that the people of the World will hate them. Therefore, they are cowardly, and stand condemned by their own lack of action and lack of commitment to our Lord Jesus Christ because they refuse to obey His commands.

This Dark World is filled with corruption from evil spirits working through naive people who are ignorant of the Truth in the Word and the meaning of life. And every person that is looking for a sign of goodness in this Dark World must fight for whatever they need to get just to survive in it to be physically safe from the evil that is so prevalent in the World. If you are part of it and love what it temporarily has to offer you in your life now, then you will have been taken advantage of by those evil spirits controlling it. Then you will lose everything you have including your chance to have eternal Life with our GOD the Father when your spirit is destroyed for accepting to live condemned in sin with Satan the prince of this Dark World. It could take a person most of their life living in the flesh to finally realize that this World offers Worldly things to enjoy in vain that end with your life in death and have nothing to offer for eternal Life.

When a person finally realizes that they are tired of living alone in this Dark World without the help of our GOD the Father, and builds up the courage to reject what this World has to offer in vain, then their mind will become clearer to realize that nothing that can be received from this World will ever bring happiness like eternal Life through having our Lord Jesus Christ can. Then that person may do what every believer in the Testimony of our GOD the Father has done and repent their sins to submit and commit their lives to our GOD the Father in the NAME of HIS Son our Lord Jesus Christ for their salvation and blessing of eternal

Chapter 14: Eternal Life is our God the Father and our Lord Jesus Christ

Life. Then because of their sanctification of believing in the Word of Truth, they may be Anointed with the Holy Spirit of our GOD the Father for HIS help through HIS Son our Lord Jesus Christ to be made a Child of GOD and to have the Right to enter the Kingdom of Heaven as a Holy Child of our GOD the Father in complete unity with THEM.

You must love the Life of having our Lord Jesus Christ more than you do living by yourself without His love in you, to prove that you deserve for Him to be living in you. His love in you will overcome all things in your life to bring you and your loved ones to eternal Life in the Kingdom of our GOD the Father. Nothing else matters in life than having eternal Life itself and believing that it was put in the Son of our GOD the Father by our GOD the Father for us to have. Our personal Spirit is who we were created to be, and we were never created to be alone. Therefore, whoever has the Son has eternal Life from Him. Accept and believe in the Testimony of our GOD the Father about HIS Son and you will have eternal Life from THEM living within you and you will never be alone again. Those who pray together in Spirit, stay together in Spirit. And we must pray in Spirit to give thanks to our GOD the Father in the NAME of our Lord Jesus Christ to stay together in Spirit with THEM in complete unity as we keep His commands to Always Love Each Other.

Believers in the Testimony of our GOD the Father will resist evil in the World because we are not part of the wickedness in this Dark World when we learn the Truth in the Word, which our GOD the Father has given us through our Lord Jesus Christ. Therefore, we must acknowledge our Lord Jesus Christ every day when we declare to everyone that our Lord is Jesus Christ and that He was sent by our GOD the Father from Heaven for our salvation. And we do that by sharing the Word of Truth in the Gospel of our Lord Jesus Christ with everyone. If He is who you believe in, then He is who you will become like. You will become like the one you believe in and follow, so be sure to follow the commands of our Lord Jesus Christ because He is exactly who you are supposed to be like for eternal Life.

- **Mathew 10:32-33 (NIV)**
  32 "Whoever acknowledges Me before others, I will also acknowledge before My Father in Heaven. 33 But whoever disowns Me before others, I will disown before My Father in Heaven.

Our Lord Jesus Christ glorified our GOD the Father, by completing what He was commanded to do by our GOD the Father. We also glorify our GOD the Father when we turn to HIM through our Lord Jesus Christ and Decide to accept HIS Word and live by HIS commands while living in the Spirit because our GOD the Father is Spirit and looks for those that live and Worship HIM in Spirit as we were created to by HIM. And since we believe in the New Covenant, we must acknowledge our Lord Jesus Christ before others to help them have salvation with eternal Life for themselves to live and give worship (in the Spirit) to our GOD the Father (through our Lord Jesus Christ).

Our Lord Jesus Christ was arrested, and the Apostles had to avoid being arrested themselves because our Lord Jesus Christ had commanded them to teach the Word and Testify about Him to the World. Our fate rests on us Deciding to believe their written Testimony that originated from the Testimony of our GOD the Father through our Lord Jesus Christ. Without learning the Word of Truth and living by the instructions that we are commanded to do in it, then we can't ever please our GOD the Father because that is living in the flesh which ends in death. Living by the commands as we are instructed to do is living in the Spirit of our Lord Jesus Christ for eternal Life. And you will know THEM when you see THEM by the blessings that they shower you within your humble life to make your path straight to our GOD the Father in the Kingdom of Heaven.

Chapter 14: Eternal Life is our God the Father and our Lord Jesus Christ

- **1 John 5:10-11 (NIV)**
10 Whoever believes in the Son of GOD accepts this Testimony. Whoever does not believe GOD has made HIM out to be a liar, because they have not believed the Testimony GOD has given about HIS Son. 11 And this is the Testimony: **GOD has given us eternal Life, and this Life is in HIS Son. Whoever has the Son has Life; Whoever does not have the Son of GOD does not have Life.**

———

Remember this and live by it.

"No one Enters eternal Life without believing the Testimony of our GOD the Father."

So, that is why the Apostles had to leave our Lord Jesus Christ alone and scatter to their separate homes to share the Testimony of our GOD the Father with the World. Now we know the Testimony of our GOD the Father and their Testimony in the Gospel of our Lord Jesus Christ. Exactly whatever our Lord Jesus Christ said would happen did happen.

Satan still did not want the Apostles and disciples to believe in our Lord Jesus Christ to spread the Holy Word of Truth to the rest of the World. Yet, the Apostles and the many disciples resisted the devil enough to overcome the wickedness of evil ones. And by the power of living in unity with the Holy Spirit of our GOD the Father, they did not fail our Lord Jesus Christ, and they stayed true in faith to the Word. Since then, the Testimony and Gospel of our Lord Jesus Christ with the Message in the Word that He taught us is written in the New Testament of the Bible for us to learn from, believe, and live by in the Spirit for eternal Life in complete unity.

It is now our time to resist against evil and stay Holy not only for ourselves but for the interest of others that will learn what we know in the Truth to help them turn to our Lord Jesus Christ for eternal life until we all see our own redemption for eternal Life in the New Kingdom by the mercy of our GOD the Father in Heaven.

- ### Ephesians 6:10-17 (NIV)
  __10__ ...be strong in the Lord and in His almighty power. __11__ Put on the Full Armor Of GOD, so that you can take your stand against the devil's schemes. __12__ For our struggle is not against flesh and blood, but against the rulers, against the authorities, against the powers of this Dark World and against the spiritual forces of evil in the Heavenly Realms. __13__ Therefore, put on the Full Armor Of GOD, so that when the day of evil comes, you may be able to stand your ground, and after you have done everything, to stand. __14__ Stand firm then, with the Breastplate of Righteousness in place, __15__ and with your feet fitted with the readiness that comes from the Gospel of Peace. __16__ In addition to all this, take up the Shield of faith, with which you can extinguish all the flaming arrows of the evil one. __17__ Take the Helmet of Salvation and the Sword of the Spirit, which is the Word of GOD.

- ### 1 Peter 5:8-11 (NIV)
  __8__ Be alert and of sober Mind. Your enemy the devil prowls around like a roaring Lion looking for someone to devour. __9__ Resist him, standing firm in the faith, because you know that the Family of Believers throughout the World is undergoing the same kind of sufferings. __10__ And the GOD of all grace, who called you to HIS eternal glory in Christ, after you have suffered a little while, will HIMSELF restore you and make you strong, firm, and steadfast. __11__ To HIM be the power for ever and ever. Amen.

Chapter 14: Eternal Life is our God the Father and our Lord Jesus Christ

- **James 4:6-7 (NIV)**
  6 But He gives us more grace. That is why Scripture says: "GOD opposes the proud but shows favor to the humble." 7 Submit yourselves, then, to GOD. Resist the devil, and he will flee from you. Come near to GOD and HE will come near to you.

And now, because of their resistance against powerful evil forces, by the power of our GOD the Father, our Lord Jesus Christ, His Apostles, and disciples were able to give us the Testimony of our GOD the Father in the written Word. And that is what we need to believe in and live by and do what it says to do now. As soon as you read it, hear it, learn it, and believe it, start living your Life by what it says to do. Then accept the Holy Spirit with the help of our Lord Jesus Christ living in you, because you belong to our GOD the Father now with HIS Seal of HIS Holy Spirit living in you, for you to follow His guidance forever. You will be recognized with HIS Seal of the Holy Spirit in you by Heavenly Creations, which is called having the mark of the Holy Spirit on your forehead that they can see by living in the Spirit Realm. The Holy Spirit radiates His power of our GOD the Father from your Body-Temple as you are now living in the Spirit Realm.

Those that have the Holy Spirit will be distinguished as different from those that don't, by having the Holy Seal. They will be seen as a Child of our GOD the Father who is protected from the evil ones and all the non-believers that will be tortured but not killed during the Fifth Trumpet by the Scorpion Locust that will be released upon the people of Earth. They will be instructed by our Lord Jesus Christ not to harm those having the Seal of our GOD the Father, the grass, any plants, or the trees; when they are released from the Abyss that will be opened by a Star like Heavenly Being, that will release the Locust to torment people on Earth for Five Months that do not have the Seal of our GOD the Father on their forehead. They will be living in fear of them and wish to die from their injuries sustained, but they will not be able to die from the pain of their torture.

The Holy Spirit, who is the Seal of our GOD the Father is your protection from evil, by the NAME of our Lord Jesus Christ because He is Lord now and He has overcome the World. He removes all darkness from within your flesh to make you a Body-temple of pure light in it, to live in complete unity with the Holy Spirit and the Spirit of our Lord Jesus Christ, therefore making you a child of our God the Father. Pray for yourself and your loved ones to be called and raised up and enter The New Kingdom and pray for those who are living in our Lord Jesus Christ during the Plagues to remain saved and safe from the Plagues. The New Kingdom is our Inheritance and your New Home now. It is your promised redemption on the Last Day for accepting the New Covenant and living by the Testimony of our GOD the Father in the New Covenant which supersedes the Old Covenant Law of Moses. By accepting the Seal of our GOD the Father, you will be remembered and protected in your darkest hour. You are never alone or left alone when you are living in complete unity.

- ### Revelation 9:1, 3-4 (NIV)
    1 The Fifth Angel sounded his Trumpet, and I saw a Star that had fallen from the sky to the Earth. The Star was given the key to the Shaft of the Abyss.

    *3 And out of the smoke Locusts came down on the Earth and were given power like that of Scorpions of the Earth. 4 They were told not to harm the grass of the Earth or any plant or tree, but only those people who did **not** have the **Seal of GOD on their Foreheads**.*

In this Testimony of the Apostle John, the Gospel of our Lord Jesus Christ declared that Satan the prince of this World stands condemned; that is Judgement. Anyone who doesn't believe in living eternal Life in

Chapter 14: Eternal Life is our God the Father and our Lord Jesus Christ

complete unity with our Lord Jesus Christ now, enough to have Him living in them, cannot cross over from death in the flesh to eternal Life in the Spirit without having Him. So be it, by their own decision to stay condemned, they are already condemned now anyway, and they have no Life after the Second Death, which only the condemned will see as their final destination that will destroy their personal Spirit.

The same certainty goes for those believers who Decided to live in the Spirit and have our Lord Jesus Christ in them: So be it, by their own Decision to have eternal Life by believing in our Lord Jesus Christ, they are already saved now. The Choice for us has already been made and given by our GOD the Father and will be offered throughout our lifetime for us to prove our faith in HIM through our Lord Jesus Christ and that we have the desire for perseverance to live and stay Holy to the day we die or the Last Day, the Lords Day, whichever comes first.

We only need to believe in THEM and Decide to accept HIS Choice for us to live Holy, to have eternal Life. It is your own Decision to accept the New Covenant of our GOD the Father to live Holy now with eternal Life for salvation, so you do not continue to stand condemned now, at this time, or after you are called up for your promise of redemption by our Lord Jesus Christ. Our lifetime in Our Body-Temple is our appointed time to prove our trust to our GOD the Father, by living in Spirit to remain Holy in our Lord Jesus Christ, HIS Son.

It is your own Decision to have eternal Life living in our Lord Jesus Christ now, and after you are raised up Holy with the Holy Spirit of our GOD the Father. You must know THEM now, to have eternal Life now and after you are raised up. Only those that reject HIS Choice for us to have eternal Life, by not living Holy by the Word; on the Last Day they will see their shame and judgment for their condemnation to the death of their Spirit, the Second Death, in accordance with their own Decision to remain condemned to death.

Our Lord Jesus Christ has overcome the World and destroyed the power of all the sin and death in it. He now has the power of eternal Life in Him, and when you have Him in you, you also have His eternal Life in you, to live Holy now. For His sacrifice, He was glorified by our GOD the Father in Heaven again and was given the power of Life in Him, to save whoever believes in Him and lives in Him, as He lives with His eternal Life in them, in complete unity. Believing in our Lord Jesus Christ is doing what He commands in the Word because your heart compels you to be motivated and follow what you believe in your heart. All your Brothers and Sisters living and always loving each other are waiting to meet you and love you as our Lord Jesus Christ lives in us and loves us all. Your loving Holy Spirit family is waiting to meet you and help you understand how to know our GOD the Father and HIS Son our Lord Jesus Christ for His eternal Life to be in you. All you have to do is Decide to accept and believe the Testimony of our GOD the Father about HIS Son.

At least, by believing this Testimony and Gospel from the Apostle John, about our Lord Jesus Christ, you are sanctified from sin now. Now it's time since you have been readied for your salvation by accepting and believing in the Testimony of our GOD the Father. Pray to our GOD the Father in your spiritual prayer, and in the NAME of His Son our Lord Jesus Christ to receive HIS Holy Spirit and the Spirit of our Lord Jesus Christ in your Body-Temple now, to remain Holy for eternal Life with THEM in complete unity. Then you may receive the Holy Spirit of our GOD the Father by HIS power enabling our Lord Jesus Christ to make you a Holy Child of our GOD the Father by forgiving you of your sins that you repent so will have the right to enter eternal Life in the New Kingdom. And by repenting your sin to our GOD the Father through our Lord Jesus Christ, in His NAME Jesus Christ, and asking HIM in spiritual prayer to receive HIS Holy Spirit as a Seal in you.

Then, since you have decided to live by the New Covenant and our Lord Jesus Christ sends you the Holy Spirit, at that time you are no longer condemned; you are now saved and you must pray in Spirit giving thanks to our GOD the Father in the NAME of our Lord Jesus Christ to remain in complete unity with THEM. They will help you remain saved and

Chapter 14: Eternal Life is our God the Father and our Lord Jesus Christ

practice learning how to follow the instructions of HIS Holy Spirit that will make your path straight to our GOD the Father in Heaven.

At your appointed time you will be called up to meet our Lord Jesus Christ in the clouds after the Holy Ones that are saved and dead in Christ. They will be raised up from their graves by the Voice of our Lord Jesus Christ first, before those living alive in Christ. Our Lord Jesus Christ foretold us how this World will end for us. Praise our GOD the Father for giving us eternal Life in HIS Son Jesus Christ our Lord, who lives within us and never fails to amaze us with HIS almighty power.

If you believe this Testimony of our GOD the Father without a doubt and have not asked to receive the Holy Spirit, do it now to receive the Holy Spirit by praying in Spirit to our GOD the Father and in the NAME of our Lord Jesus Christ, and it will be done immediately without delay through our Lord Jesus Christ. And now, if you have prayed in Spirit and received HIS Holy Spirit, the Seal Testifies that you are a Child of our GOD the Father and you will be protected by our Lord Jesus Christ because you are included in our Lord Jesus Christ from the first time you heard and believed in Him. For that, you are a son or daughter that belongs to our GOD the Father and will be led by HIS Holy Spirit to live by HIS Word of Truth. They will protect you and your children if you are a parent. They will bless the entire family that you love and pray for in Spirit because they want you to know that THEY are Blessing yours with the love that your heart cries out for to protect THEM. Be saved and stay saved, and help others turn to our Lord Jesus Christ to teach them to Always Love Each Other.

This is the Word, from our GOD the Father through our Lord Jesus Christ, and it is the Truth.

- **Ephesians 1:13-14 (NIV)**
  13 And you also were included in Christ when you heard the Message of Truth, the Gospel of your salvation. When you

believed, you were marked in Him with a Seal, the promised Holy Spirit, 14 who is a deposit guaranteeing our Inheritance until the redemption of those who are GOD'S possessions— To the Praise of HIS Glory.

With our Lord Jesus Christ living in us, we have no sin anymore and will not be judged on the Last Day, which is the Judgement Day. On that day, believers that have been living by their Spirit, Worshipping in Spirit, being guided by the Holy Spirit, with the Spirit of our Lord Jesus Christ in themselves, in complete unity, will receive what is called the Crown of Life, the Crown of Glory, or the Crown of Righteousness, at the Holy Throne of our Lord Jesus Christ. That is the reward that believers will receive at what is called the "BEMA Seat", Judgement Seat, Judgement Seat of Jesus Christ, Throne of our Lord Jesus Christ. The believers in Him will not see Judgement or shame on His Throne. This is the Last Day, the Day we will HONOR Him in His Glory and receive our redemption for doing good while living Holy in our Body-Temple and for Deciding to live in the Spirit, in complete unity.

Judgement Day is also reserved for the wicked and non-believers to be judged for the evil, sin, and bad they Decided to live by in their body, and for rejecting the Testimony of our GOD the Father Concerning HIS Son, our Lord Jesus Christ. That day they will be gathered and taken to their place for standing condemned, to be executed out of existence, for the sin they kept committing in their body. Just like detached Vine Branches that are cut off by our GOD the Father for not Bearing Fruit. They will be gathered to be completely destroyed and cease to exist; they will die. That is the final death for all the evil spirits; and the Second Death for those that had bodies of flesh, because the body dies when the Spirit is separated from it. Since they did stand condemned on Earth, as they decided to live without our Lord Jesus Christ, they will be taken to the place for their final destination, the death of their personal Spirit. That is Judgement for non-believers, the final and Second Death.

Chapter 14: Eternal Life is our God the Father and our Lord Jesus Christ

- **Revelation 21:8 (NIV)**
  8 But the Cowardly, the Unbelieving, the Vile, the Murderers, the Sexually Immoral, those who Practice Magic Arts, the Idolaters, and all Liars—They will be consigned to the Fiery Lake of burning sulfur. This is the Second Death."

By their final execution from being judged by our Lord Jesus Christ, we will be protected from evil forever. And those that lived Holy in complete unity with our Lord Jesus Christ and has His eternal Life in them will not be judged, for they have no sin in them and lived Holy from being forgiven by our GOD the Father, through our Lord Jesus Christ. They will be given the Crown of Glory, also referred to as the Crown of Life, the Crown of Righteousness.

This is the Word, and it is the Truth.

- **1 Peter 5:4 (NIV)**
  4 And when the Chief Sheppard appears, (Jesus Christ) you will receive the Crown of Glory that will never fade away.

- **2 Corinthians 5 (NIV)**
  10 For we must all appear before the Judgement Seat of Christ, so that each of us may receive what is due us for the things done while in the body, whether Good or Bad.

At that time believers in Christ Jesus will not be judged or put to shame because they have no sin or bad in them to be judged by. They are already forgiven and have been living Holy with the Spirit of our Lord Jesus Christ in them, in unity within their Body-Temple with their own personal Spirit and the Holy Spirit of our GOD the Father all in complete unity. And our Advocate, the Holy Spirit of our GOD the Father will Testify with our personal Spirit as One, that we are a Holy Child of our GOD the Father.

———

- Hebrews 10:9-10, 18 (NIV)
  9 Then He (Jesus Christ) said, "Here I am, I have come to do Your will." (GOD the Father) He (Jesus Christ) sets aside the First (Old Covenant) to establish the Second. (New Covenant) 10 And by that will (GOD the Father), we have been made Holy through the sacrifice of the Body of Jesus Christ once for all.

  18 And where these have been forgiven, sacrifice for sin is no longer necessary.

———

The good deeds we have done and will do in our Body-Temple will be remembered because we have lived in complete unity with our Lord Jesus Christ. As our Lord Jesus Christ has Testified about the Holy Spirit, the Holy Spirit will Testify with our Spirit that we are faithful Children belonging to our GOD the Father. And for that, we will receive the Crown of Life, the Crown of Glory, the Crown of Righteousness. Being Crowned is a symbol for recognition as a Child of our GOD the Father. Our reward is to be recognized in Heaven by all Beings, as eternal living Spirit Servants of our GOD the Father with HIS Son our Lord Jesus Christ, living by HIS will. We will be recognized as we were created differently than the Angels in Heaven because we were created in flesh and Spirit which are contrary to each other.

We are different because we have to fight a Holy war within ourselves to overcome our own sinful desires of our own flesh and win over our own flesh, by accepting to live by our own Spirit and by our own Decision to accept the gift of eternal Life through our Lord Jesus Christ

Chapter 14: Eternal Life is our God the Father and our Lord Jesus Christ

which was given by the mercy of our GOD the Father. HIS New Covenant for us is to reconcile all things to HIMSELF through the Blood Sacrifice of HIS only begotten Son, our Lord Jesus Christ.

We will become the image of our Lord Jesus Christ, the only begotten Son of our GOD the Father in the Heavenly Realm, who sits at the Right Hand of our GOD the Father, the MOST HIGH, and creator of all things. HE is reconciling all things to HIMSELF through our Lord Jesus Christ, and we are here as Servants to help HIM in any way HE asks of us without question or doubt. Therefore, we will stay fearless without a doubt to our death in the flesh which will happen anyway, by having faith in the power of our Lord Jesus Christ that will raise us up after our death in the flesh anyway. Know this, that you are alive in our Lord Jesus Christ now to be known by Him with a hope to die in Christ to be remembered by Him as one of the dead in Christ. Then at the appointed time, He will raise us up with an imperishable Spirit Body to meet Him and your loved ones once again to live forever with them.

But, for the non-believers, they will be judged to die in the Second Death by their Decision to not accept to believe in the Testimony of our GOD the Father. Any good that non-believers did in their bodies will not be remembered to help them escape their final destruction from the Second Death for their bad, selfish, and evil deeds.

By having the Seal of our GOD the Father living in you, you are promised by HIM that you will inherit eternal Life in the Kingdom of our GOD the Father when you are redeemed on the Last Day, the Lord's Day and you will never be harmed by the evil one. That is the reward and redemption promised to those that live Holy in their Body-Temple now. And by believing and asking for the Holy Spirit from our GOD the Father in the NAME of our Lord Jesus Christ and accepting our Lord Jesus Christ to live in you and you in Him; that brings you into complete unity and Holy with THEM for eternal Life now. So, it shall be done for you because you believe in having a spiritual relationship in the NAME of our Lord

Jesus Christ in your Body-Temple now and before the Last Day when our Lord Jesus Christ will raise you up to Heaven to redemption for the good in you.

The Judgement for those condemned that will be consigned to the Lake of Fire for their final destruction to be executed for their bad ways, is for those that rejected our Lord Jesus Christ and Decided not to believe in Him and not to live united with Him in their body. They will be destroyed with Hades and Sheol, and at last Death, by being thrown into the Lake of Fire of burning fire and sulfur. They will be no more and there will be no more death by their final destruction of death. That is how it will be after the end of their existence. They Decided not to live Holy in their body and to stay condemned, the way they were condemned anyway. Therefore, they will be raised up to the Judgement Seat, and show up with sin, evil, and unholy in their Spirit that kept them standing condemned with Satan and his demons that have been waiting to be executed out of existence at their appointed time for their transgression against our almighty GOD the Father of all creation.

Sharing these letters and messages of the written Word with others daily shows that we "Always Love Each Other" to help others live, love, and remain in our Lord Jesus Christ daily, for the Holy Life in Him to be in us all. And it is a reminder for every believer to keep His commands in the Word every day to "Always Love One Another". Remember the commands given by our Lord Jesus Christ but remember the First and Greatest Command and the Second that is like it.

- Love GOD with all your Soul, your Heart, and your Mind.
- Love your Neighbor as yourself.

   Do:
- Honor Your Mother and Father.
- Love your Neighbor as yourself.

   Do not:
- Murder.
- Steal.

Chapter 14: Eternal Life is our God the Father and our Lord Jesus Christ

- Commit Adultery.
- Bear False Testimony.

———

The New Command: -**Always Love Each Other.**

If you keep the New Command, you will keep all the other commands by your Nature of goodness. We must practice now as we learn how to Always Love Each Other because that is what our Lord Jesus Christ commanded us to do. By keeping true to His New Command, we show that we love Him and our GOD the Father to our last breath on Earth, which will happen for everyone who believes. We will all take our last breath on Earth anyway without fail. Get your mindset right with our Lord Jesus Christ and fix yourself with His help. We are not of this World; we are of the Heavenly Realms of the Spirit and the will of our GOD the Father is for us to have eternal Life with HIM forever through our Lord Jesus Christ. Stay saved now and live in complete unity with THEM for eternal Life now and after your resurrection from this World.

And This Is Our Prayer:

We ask You in prayer as we give thanks to You, our GOD the Father, in the NAME of your Son Jesus Christ, for loving us and saving us through our Lord Jesus Christ, your only begotten Son. We have faith that our Lord Jesus Christ will present us to You in Heaven joyful and Holy, because of Your will to forgive us of all our sins so we will not see judgment or shame on the Last Day.

We ask and pray in Spirit in the Holy NAME our Lord Jesus Christ.

Chapter 14: Eternal Life is our GOD the Father and our Lord Jesus Christ

John 17:1-12 NIV

<u>1</u> "After Jesus said this, He looked toward Heaven and prayed: "Father, the hour has come. Glorify Your Son, that Your Son may glorify You.

<u>2</u> For You granted Him Authority over all people that He might give eternal Life to all those You have given Him.

<u>3</u> **Now this is eternal Life: That they know You, the only True GOD, and Jesus Christ, whom You have sent.**

<u>4</u> I have brought You glory on Earth by finishing the work You gave Me to do.

<u>5</u> And now, Father, glorify Me in Your presence with the glory I had with You before the World began."

<u>6</u> "I have revealed You to those whom You gave Me out of the World. They were Yours; You gave them to Me and they have obeyed Your Word.

<u>7</u> Now they know that everything You have given Me comes from You.

<u>8</u> For I gave them the Words You gave Me and they accepted them. They knew with certainty that I came from You, and they believed that You sent Me.

Chapter 14: Eternal Life is our God the Father and our Lord Jesus Christ

9 I pray for them. I am not praying for the World, but for those You have given Me, for they are Yours.

10 All I have is Yours, and all You have is mine. And glory has come to Me through them."

11 I will remain in the World no longer, but they are still in the World, and I am coming to You. Holy Father, protect them by the power of Your NAME, the NAME You gave Me, so that they may be One as WE are One.

12 While I was with them, I protected them and kept them safe by that NAME You gave Me. (Jesus Christ) None has been lost except the one doomed to destruction (Judas Iscariot) so that scripture would be fulfilled.

❖ Notice:

Our Lord Jesus Christ prays to our GOD the Father. He prays because our GOD the Father is also His LORD, and GOD, and His Father. He is our living GOD and our Father, the ETERNAL ONE. He is the source of power, of all power dwelling in our Lord Jesus Christ, and through Christ Jesus, our Lord was given the power for everything to be created, including the Heavens and Earth. Everything that was created with the power of our GOD the Father was made through our Lord Jesus Christ. Therefore, we may say, that before anything was made, that could be made, was made through our Lord Jesus Christ, after He was created first, as the first-born Son of our GOD the Father.

In the beginning, our Lord Jesus Christ was the first created and only Son, that is, He was the first Spirit with our GOD the Father; the first and only begotten divine Son, He was created as the WORD of GOD with the same nature of our GOD the Father, in the same divine Spirit likeness of our GOD the Father, in Spirit. The same divine nature of love is the likeness that our GOD the Father is, who HIMSELF is love, and that nature was created in HIS Son by our GOD the Father.

Our Lord Jesus Christ reveals in prayer that all His authority given to Him was given to Him by our GOD the Father, so that He may give eternal life to those on Earth who believe in Him and believe that He was sent to us from our GOD the Father. That is written in the Testimony of our GOD the Father for us to believe in with certainty. Let the Holy Spirit write it in your heart, and He will miraculously remind you of the Word you learned from the scriptures to keep you saved away from sin in everything you say and do to become the image of our Lord Jesus Christ. We bow our knees to our Lord and Savior to honor Him by His NAME as we pray in Spirit to give thanks to our GOD the Father in Heaven. Even though our Lord Jesus Christ was given everything that belongs to our GOD the Father; and our Lord Jesus Christ has the same perfect divine nature of love as our GOD the Father; our Lord Jesus Christ never, ever, considered Himself the equal to His creator and Father who is also our GOD and Father.

Our Lord Jesus Christ took His position as a servant to our GOD the Father and fulfilled all the prophecies written in the scriptures concerning Himself at that time. And He kept the commands that He was given by our GOD the Father to accomplish on Earth to show the World that He loves our GOD the Father by His words and deeds. And we must do as our Lord Jesus Christ has done, as an example of how to live a Holy Life now, in complete unity with Him. And we are constantly becoming transformed into the image of our Lord Jesus Christ, with ever increasing enlightenment, while living Holy now in complete unity with Him, as we keep His commands by our words and deeds that we do and say with our faith in THEM.

The first two Humans, (Adam and Eve), were made in the image of our GOD the Father which is in HIS perfect nature of love and Truth without sin, the same as our Lord Jesus Christ was made perfect in the same nature as our GOD the Father. We must understand that is how we were intended to be in our nature. We were created perfect by our GOD the

Chapter 14: Eternal Life is our God the Father and our Lord Jesus Christ

Father to live in HIS presence without sin in us just like the Angels in Heaven are perfect and Holy servants of our GOD the Father and now submit and commit to our Lord Jesus Christ who has been given Authority over all things in Heaven and Earth. But as soon as lies were told to the first two Humans by the Father of Lies, Satan, and they believed in him; sin was committed by them believing in Satan, and that transgression and disgrace separates us from our GOD the Father in Heaven.

When his words, which were contrary to the command of GOD, were believed in by the first two Humans they were transformed out of perfection because living with sin is living outside of the protection from the Holy power of Life that our GOD the Father provides for eternal Life. They came out from living Holy with HIM, and into living in sin without HIM. That is the same sin that Satan has in himself and the demons that make him condemned and doomed for destruction. They transgressed against our GOD the Father by disobeying HIS Command to abstain from taking fruit from the Tree of Knowledge, which they were warned and commanded by our GOD the Father not to take from the Tree of Knowledge or they would surely die. Our GOD the Father never makes idle threats, HIS Word is fact and in effect the moment HE speaks. Do not be confused, always believe HIS Word and believe HIS Testimony concerning the Life that HE put in our Lord Jesus Christ for us to have eternal Life in us now on Earth as it is in Heaven and live by HIS commands.

The first Two Humans on Earth and many angels from Heaven listened to Satan's lies and believed his words contrary to what they were warned against; and by that, they are making our GOD the Father out to be a liar, which HE is not a liar and has no need for liars. That behavior of believing a lie is a sin in itself. Satan has no truth in himself, and he is the father of lies that now stands condemned for causing the World to be disgraced in sin. Now, all the descendants of the first two in Humanity on Earth stand condemned with Satan by living in sin with him. The whole World is condemned, yet our GOD the Father has made for us the Covenant of the Spirit of Life through believing and accepting HIS Son our Lord Jesus Christ. That is HIS Choice to give us a Way out of condemnation and death to cross over to eternal Life.

Sin is what separates us from our GOD the Father and HE will destroy everything and anything associated with sin to do HIS will, which is to make us Holy Children in HIS sight and live with us. Therefore, we must denounce Satan and sin to rid ourselves of him and all his ways of sin. And we must believe in our Heart and declare with our Mouth that our Lord Jesus Christ is our Lord who was sent to us by our GOD the Father for our salvation to have eternal Life again.

Our GOD the Father has given us the gift of Life through our Lord Jesus Christ giving us a way out of condemnation, so we may persevere from having sin in us starting in this lifetime in our Body-Temple now and so we will never see the Second Death. Those who do not accept the mercy in the New Covenant of the Spirit from our GOD the Father to have Life on Earth now will surely see Judgement, doom, and destruction in the Second Death to pass away before Death itself is destroyed forever.

Our GOD the Father does not lie, and HE sent our Lord Jesus Christ as a Sin Offering to reconcile Mankind to HIMSELF, to make us live Holy in Spirit as HE initially intended for us to live with HIM in the Paradise that HE provided for us. Without sin, we will have the same Spirit nature of love and the mindset that our Lord Jesus Christ has living in us. Our Lord Jesus Christ describes the nature, He wants us to become, and that is in His own image. Therefore, we must strive every moment of our short lives on Earth to become His image and to Always Love Each Other, as much as He is the image of our GOD the Father. We must Always Love Each Other as THEY love us in complete unity within us. Exactly as His Word says we must do.

This is the Word, and it is the Truth.

Chapter 14: Eternal Life is our God the Father and our Lord Jesus Christ

- **Philippians 2:5-6 (NIV)**
  5 In your relationships with one another, have the same Mindset as Christ Jesus: 6 Who, being in very nature GOD, did not consider equality with GOD…

Our almighty GOD the Father has the power to bring our Lord Jesus Christ back to Life in a Spirit Body after His death, with the power of HIS Holy Spirit that comes out from our GOD the Father. The same Holy Spirit that will transform us back to Life with a new imperishable Spirit Body, when it is our appointed time to be redeemed, as our Lord Jesus Christ was redeemed and lives Holy in the presence of our GOD the Father in the Highest Place, and He sits at the Right-Hand side of our GOD the Father in Heaven.

- **1 Corinthians 15:42 (NIV)**
  42 So will it be with the resurrection of the dead. The body that is sown is perishable, (in Flesh - Body) *But, it is raised imperishable.* (in Spirit- Body)

We must declare that we believe with all our Hearts, Souls, and Minds to be sanctified as we declare with our Mouths to others that our Lord is Jesus Christ to be saved. All the people who decided to live by the Spirit who are in complete unity with our Lord Jesus Christ believe in the Testimony of our GOD the Father and live by it by doing what HIS Word tells us to do and Always Love Each Other. And to do that, we must take the time we need each day to talk it out with others and teach them the Word of Truth that we know, to help them have our Lord Jesus Christ working in them for eternal Life. There is no other way to salvation except through the One and only Lord Jesus Christ. He is the Son of our GOD the Father, who put eternal Life in Him for us to have when we accept His Spirit in our Body-Temple to become One with THEM in Spirit.

- **ROMANS 10:8-13 (NIV)**
  8... "The Word is near you; it is in your Mouth and in your Heart," that is, the message concerning faith that we proclaim: 9 If you declare with your Mouth, Jesus is Lord, and believe in your Heart that GOD raised Him from the dead, you will be saved. 10 For it is with your Heart that you believe and are Justified, and it is with your Mouth that you profess your faith and are saved. 11 As scripture says, "Anyone who believes in Him will never be put to shame." 12 For there is no difference between Jew and Gentile— The same Lord is Lord of all and blesses all who call on Him, 13 for, "Everyone who calls on (Jesus Christ) *the NAME of the Lord will be saved."*

Therefore, our Lord Jesus Christ said, "Eternal life is to know the only True GOD the Father and our Lord Jesus Christ." Our Lord Jesus Christ revealed four important points of believers that please our GOD the Father.

- They believe and obey the Word of Truth with the New Covenant and the commands in it.

- They know everything given to our Lord Jesus Christ comes from our GOD the Father.

- They accept to live by the Word given to them through our Lord Jesus Christ and everything that He learned from our GOD the Father.

- They believe the Testimony of our GOD the Father and know for certain that our GOD the Father sent our Lord Jesus Christ from HIS presence in Heaven to save us from condemnation on Earth.

Chapter 14: Eternal Life is our God the Father and our Lord Jesus Christ

Our GOD the Father gave HIS Son, the Anointed One, our Lord Jesus Christ to us with the power of eternal Life in Him to be living in us. And anyone that calls on the NAME of our Lord Jesus Christ and comes to Him for eternal Life is given to Him to be forgiven of all their sin to be made spiritually Holy in their Body-Temple now on Earth and for eternal Life. After we are raised to Life by our Lord Jesus Christ and into our new imperishable Spirit-Body, we will appear Holy with our Lord Jesus Christ in the presence of our GOD the Father to be presented to HIM Holy and in Spirit.

Our Lord Jesus Christ acknowledges the power of the created NAME He was given when He was glorified by our GOD the Father before the Earth was made. And when our Lord Jesus Christ prayed to our GOD the Father, He referred to His own given NAME as a significant NAME of power and that it belongs to our GOD the Father who created His NAME; like an item of significant value that only our GOD the Father, the Creator of the NAME has the power to give to HIS Son. And just like our Lord Jesus Christ, our Names have significant value to our GOD the Father, so much that HE has them written in Heaven in the Book of Life that belongs to our GOD the Father. Keep your Name Holy and rejoice in song and prayer giving thanks to our GOD the Father, in the NAME of His only begotten Son our Lord Jesus Christ because you and your Name that is written in Heaven all belong to our GOD the Father.

We completely belong to HIM when we submit and commit ourselves to HIM by praying in Spirit when we first believe HIS Testimony. And, at that time we were marked in HIS Son, our Lord Jesus Christ. We are marked in Him with the Seal of our GOD the Father. HIS Seal is by having HIS Holy Spirit that is living in us now with our personal Spirit and with the Spirit of our Lord Jesus Christ in complete unity.

- **Luke 10:20 (NIV)**
    [20] However, do not rejoice that the spirits submit to you, but rejoice that your Names are written in Heaven."

And our GOD the Father created the very NAME, Jesus Christ, to personify the perfect divinity of HIS Son the WORD of Life, who is HIS only begotten Son, our Lord Jesus Christ. The only One that the NAME Jesus Christ completely personifies. Since we were created by our GOD the Father, we belong to HIM and we have to Decide to submit and commit ourselves as servants to HIM to show ourselves to be deserving of the Choice that HE made for us, to have eternal Life and the love HE gives to us, through HIS Son living in us, in complete unity.

Our GOD the Father gave us eternal Life by the Blood Sacrifice of HIS only begotten Son to reconcile us to HIMSELF. No one can enter eternal Life without believing in the Testimony of our GOD the Father as the Truth to live by. It is in HIS Word of Truth and it explains the New Covenant of the Spirit, which frees us from certain death by condemnation, to bring us HIS will and Choice to give us eternal Life if we should so Decide to accept to live by what HIS Word says, to keep HIS commands that our Lord Jesus Christ taught us to live by in His message to us. And by accepting the Baptism of Spirit and Fire into us, the Holy Spirit will write the entire message of our Lord Jesus Christ into our hearts for us to boldly share with others who desire to have the Life of our Lord Jesus Christ living in themselves.

The Holy Spirit will help fire you up by inspiring you with the words to live and speak the Word of Truth He teaches you. It is truly a miracle to see and feel the Holy Spirit at work through yourself every day to make you more righteous and faithful. You will feel it in your Heart, Mind, and Soul, as the radiating power of love - from the Holy Spirit - flows through you to help others reconcile to our GOD the Father through our Lord Jesus Christ. Don't be surprised when it finally hits you, when you least expect it, and you know for certain by the powerful feeling of Power, Love, Self-Control, and joy that you are saved by the power of the Holy Spirit from within you. Even with tears in your eyes, it is the time to rejoice, rejoice with song and happiness that our Lord Jesus Christ has spoken to you in a way that only you can understand and feel at that

Chapter 14: Eternal Life is our God the Father and our Lord Jesus Christ

moment in time. That is a moment for you to keep and share as your Testimony, that the Holy Spirit is letting you know you are on the right track with Him. Hold on to that memory and pray that you remember it because it is your Testimony to remind yourself and share with others if you should so desire, and to keep for yourself to grow stronger in the love of our Lord Jesus Christ and in the love of our GOD the Father for the Life that will last forever.

Always believe and strengthen your faith when you positively know that the power of our Lord Jesus Christ is alive and working within you to make you more worthy of His love and stronger in faith. You will know for certain that our GOD the Father has mercy on you and that you are included in our Lord Jesus Christ forever. Your burden of sin and all the hurt that goes with it will be lifted out of your Soul to never torment you again because the immense power of our Lord Jesus Christ has destroyed the effect of sin on you permanently and forever. No one can ever use that sin against you, not even yourself, to make you feel or think you are unworthy of eternal Life, because only our Lord Jesus Christ is Judge and Executioner with the power of Life over the power of sin and death to take away the effects sin had on you.

And with that love, give all that you have, with all your Heart, Mind, and Soul to live by the commands to stay Holy with the Holy Spirit and the Spirit of our Lord Jesus Christ in you. Believe in the power of our Lord Jesus Christ. Do not look back and worry about the sin that you were forgiven for by our Lord Jesus Christ. Strike it from your Mind by the power in the NAME of our Lord Jesus Christ because He has given you the righteous requirement of a Holy Life enough to deserve to enter eternal Life in the New Kingdom as a Holy Child of our GOD the Father.

At the time you first believed, you have crossed over to eternal Life already and live in the Spirit Realm now, in complete unity with our Lord Jesus Christ in you. And if you ever need to check yourself or anyone for that matter to see if you honestly believe that you are saved in our Lord Jesus Christ, just ask yourself if you believe the Testimony of our GOD the Father. The Testimony HE gave concerning HIS Son for us to know and believe in explains HIS New Covenant with us and for us. As it is written in the Word, everyone who believes in our GOD the Father believes in HIS Testimony concerning our Lord Jesus Christ HIS Son. If your answer is yes and you live by it without a doubt, you undeniably have eternal Life if you keep His commands. That is your Testimony to remember and share as necessary to help others.

This is the Word of our GOD the Father given to our Lord Jesus Christ for us to believe in, and it is the Truth.

———

- **1 John 5 (NIV)**
  11 And this is the Testimony: -GOD has given us eternal Life, and this Life is in HIS Son. 12 Whoever has the Son has Life; whoever does not have the Son of GOD does not have Life.

———

Everyone is condemned unless they believe and accept to live in complete unity with our Lord Jesus Christ. Anyone living in complete unity now has eternal Life in their Body-Temple and their good deeds will be remembered with the Holy Spirit as our witness together with our personal Spirit. Our GOD the Father gave us all to our Lord Jesus Christ to be our Teacher, Savior, and Lord, so that we may believe in our GOD the Father and HIS Son to be free of sin now, to live Holy in Spirit now.

Our GOD the Father sent our Lord Jesus Christ for our sanctification and salvation, so that we may be brought up as a Child of GOD the Father, to be with THEM now on Earth and later in HIS Kingdom because HE loves us and wants us to be with HIM, so HE can care for us with HIS love in us. That is why we must be reconciled to our GOD the Father without sin; to be made Holy by the righteousness in us by having our Lord Jesus Christ in us, and then be raised Up Holy with HIS Holy Spirit to HIMSELF by HIS Son, our Lord Jesus Christ.

Humankind was first created Holy in paradise to live in the presence of

Chapter 14: Eternal Life is our God the Father and our Lord Jesus Christ

our GOD the Father. We must accept our Lord Jesus Christ to be forgiven of the sins in us to be made Holy, as we were intended to live Holy, so we may live in the presence of our GOD the Father and no longer be separated from Him by the sin in us. Only through and by our Lord Jesus Christ can we first be transformed into Holy Human Beings within our Body-Temple living in the Spirit with the Holy Spirit and the Spirit of our Lord Jesus Christ, until He Calls us UP to Himself and transforms us into imperishable Spirit Bodies to live in the Spirit Realm with Him in the presence of our GOD the Father forever.

We call on the NAME of our Lord Jesus Christ in our own language, in our own tongue, as it is spoken and written in the Bible that we learn from. The NAME of our Lord Jesus Christ is a Holy NAME that will invoke the power of our GOD the Father when you pray to HIM in Spirit, in the NAME of HIS Son, Christ Jesus. That is praying through our Lord Jesus Christ and honoring Him while giving thanks to our GOD the Father. HE hears our prayers to protect us at HIS will through our Lord Jesus Christ. All glory be to our GOD the Father. Our GOD the Father searches your heart and knows what you want to say before you speak. And if you don't know what to ask in prayer, HIS Holy Spirit in your heart will intercede for you and speak for you in Wordless Groans to our GOD the Father.

- ## Romans 8:26-27 (NIV)
    26 In the same way, the Spirit helps us in our weakness. We do not know what we ought to pray for, but the Spirit Himself intercedes for us through Wordless Groans. 27 And (GOD the Father) He who searches our hearts knows the Mind of the Spirit, because the Spirit intercedes for GOD'S People in accordance with the will of GOD.

Seventy-two disciples rejoiced as they told our Lord Jesus Christ, that even the demons submitted to them in His NAME. They saw and felt the power in the NAME of our Lord Jesus Christ when they called on His NAME to glorify our GOD the Father. That was when they went from town to town to teach the Gospel and Testify about our Lord Jesus Christ and the Word written in the New Covenant. They cast out demons in the NAME of our Lord Jesus Christ. And by the power in the NAME of our Lord Jesus Christ, the evil demons did what they were told to do by the disciples. Because our Lord Jesus Christ gave them the authority that enabled them to do those things when He was with them. Just like He gave authority to His Twelve disciples to do those things that prove He is the Son, sent by our GOD the Father.

- ### Mathew 10 (NIV)
  1 Jesus called His Twelve disciples to Him and gave them authority to drive out impure spirits and to heal every disease and sickness.

Yet, our Lord Jesus Christ told the disciples, do not rejoice that the spirits submitted to them in His NAME, but they should rejoice that their own Names are written in Heaven. That is how important your Name is to our GOD the Father. As a believer in our Lord Jesus Christ, your Name is so important that it is written in Heaven, in the Book of Life, for you to enter eternal Life in the Kingdom of our GOD the Father and have a place there forever.

And as it is written for Satan the devil and his fallen angels, there was no longer found any place for them in Heaven. They were cast out of Heaven and thrown down to the Earth for a short time compared to eternity as we know it. They can't enter Heaven anymore and they will not have eternal Life anymore as they were initially intended to have, the same as we were initially intended to have eternal Life. Because they turned against our GOD the Father by using his evil ways of sin, lies, and confusion to keep us living in sin. They stand condemned and

Chapter 14: Eternal Life is our God the Father and our Lord Jesus Christ

anyone that does not live by the commands of our Lord Jesus Christ also stand condemned already with Satan and by their own Decision they cannot enter eternal Life in the Kingdom of Heaven any more than Satan, which is never again for him and his followers.

Therefore, all non-believers are condemned, as it is with Judas Iscariot who turned against our Lord Jesus Christ, because they are subject to doom and destruction the same as Satan and Judas for their Decision and status of living in condemnation. This event about Satan is written in the Book of Revelations and has already happened, and our Lord Jesus Christ revealed who did it because He saw it happen when He was in Heaven to see it happen, just as He told the Seventy-Two disciples how it happened by the power of our GOD the Father.

- **Revelation 12 (NIV)**
  7 Then War broke out in Heaven. Michael and His Angels fought against the dragon (Satan)*, and the dragon and his angels fought back. 8 But* (Satan) *he was not strong enough, and they lost their place in Heaven. 9 The great dragon was hurled down—That Ancient Serpent called the devil, or Satan, who leads the whole World astray. He was hurled to the Earth, and his angels with him.*

- **Luke 10:18 (NIV)**
  18 He (Jesus Christ) replied, "I saw Satan fall like lightning from Heaven.

Satan now stands condemned, and that is Judgement. And by the power of our GOD the Father, HIS Messenger the Archangel Michael carried out HIS Command to cast out Satan and the angels that followed him. And it happened as fast as lightning from Heaven to Earth. No one can stand against the will of the Words and commands of our GOD the Father. And those that follow Satan to practice sin will all be doomed to destruction, which means condemned and executed, at their appointed time and place. That is why it can be said that the whole World is condemned except those that have our Lord Jesus Christ as it is in the Testimony of our GOD the Father.

Our Lord Jesus Christ asked our GOD the Father to protect us by the power of the NAME He was given, because only by our Lord Jesus Christ can we be sanctified to receive the Holy Spirit for salvation and be given protection from evil. The NAME of our Lord Jesus Christ is so relevant to believers following our Lord Jesus Christ, that He tells us to pray in Spirit to our GOD the Father and ask of HIM in the NAME of our Lord Jesus Christ. We have HIS Holy Spirit in us that was sent to us from our GOD the Father, by the NAME of our Lord Jesus Christ.

- **Philippians 2:9-11 (NIV)**
    9 Therefore GOD exalted Him to the Highest Place and gave Him the NAME that is above every Name, 10 that at the NAME of Jesus every knee should bow, in Heaven and on Earth and Under the Earth, 11 and every tongue acknowledge that Jesus Christ is Lord, to the glory of GOD the Father.

Rejoice! Because you are so loved by our GOD the Father, that HE sent you HIS Holy Spirit in the NAME of HIS only begotten Son Jesus Christ, to help guide you and save you from sin and condemnation and to protect you from the evil one. While you are living Holy on Earth you are protected by the power of His NAME Jesus Christ who is living in complete unity with you.

Chapter 14: Eternal Life is our God the Father and our Lord Jesus Christ

- **COLOSSIANS 3:17 (NIV)**
  17 And whatever you do, whether in word or deed, do it all in the NAME of the Lord Jesus Christ, giving thanks to GOD the Father through Him.

And now you know the power in the NAME of our Lord "Jesus Christ" created by our GOD the Father.

- **John 5:24 (NIV)**
  24 "Very truly I tell you, whoever hears My Word and believes HIM who sent Me has eternal Life and will not be judged but has crossed over from death to Life.

- **John 5:26-29 (NIV)**
  26 For as the Father has Life in HIMSELF, so HE has granted the Son also to have Life in Himself. 27 And HE has given Him Authority to Judge because He is the Son of Man. 28 "Do not be amazed at this, for a time is coming when all who are in their graves will hear His Voice 29 and come out—those who have done what is "good" will rise to Live, and those who have done what is "evil" will rise to be condemned.

These scriptures in the Word elaborate in many ways that our Lord Jesus Christ supports and explains the Testimony of our GOD the Father concerning Him and the New Covenant. Only the ones that believe in the Testimony of our GOD the Father and keep the commands that HIS Son has given to us are doing good and will rise to Live. Those who refuse to believe in our Lord Jesus Christ and refuse to live in the Spirit by the Word, are condemned already in the flesh by their own Decision.

And not believing and living by the Testimony of our GOD the Father is evil, and those ones will rise to be condemned to their doom and destruction.

As a believer in our Lord Jesus Christ, asking and giving thanks to our GOD the Father in the NAME of our Lord Jesus Christ is giving glory to our GOD the Father through our Lord Jesus Christ. And those that believe in our Lord Jesus Christ and accept to live by the Word in the Spirit have crossed over from death to Life already, by receiving the Holy Spirit and living in complete unity now by their own Decision. We are already saved as we help our Lord Jesus Christ make our GOD the Father known to the World while awaiting the appointed time of our redemption with the Seal of the Holy Spirit from our GOD the Father and the Spirit of our Lord Jesus Christ within us. By knowing THEM we have eternal Life in us now.

Chapter 14: Eternal Life is our God the Father and our Lord Jesus Christ

<u>*And This Is Our Prayer:*</u>

We pray in Spirit to You, our GOD the Father, and we thank You for sending Your only begotten Son Jesus Christ to save us with Your Word of Truth.

We believe in our Hearts and profess with our Mouths that eternal Life is knowing You and our Lord Jesus Christ as our Lord and Savior.

Our hope is to remain in Your love with Your Holy Spirit and the Spirit of Your Son Jesus Christ in complete unity so that we may make our home with You in the New Kingdom.

We ask of You in the NAME of Your Son, our Lord Jesus Christ.

Chapter 15: Unify with our GOD the Father and our Lord Jesus Christ

This is the fifteenth chapter of this fifteen-day cycle of scriptures and prayers. We start over at chapter one to teach the Gospel - and the Word of Truth - with the Testimony of our GOD the Father about our Lord Jesus Christ for our sanctification and salvation with our Lord Jesus Christ in complete unity in Spirit. When we study these chapters with our family and friends, as we pray in Spirit to contemplate the subjects that will arise, we will be reminded about our testimony and Life experiences that will bring new inspiration to those living in Spirit with the Holy Spirit of GOD.

This will bring our family closer together as a loving family that understands the meaning of life. Then share your gift with others you meet who may be looking for a way to learn the Truth for themselves at their own convenience to get to know GOD and about the Choice that our GOD has given to the people of the world as a gift for us to be inspired with eternal life through having HIS Son in Spirit within ourselves.

GOD gave us HIS Word of Truth, but very few understand how to live by it as we are commanded to do, and they miss out on knowing the inspiration for eternal life to become completely inspired living in Spirit. This is how each one of us can feed the hungry for the Word of our God the Father, with the power of GOD. This is our time to prove that we can always love each other with the Word of Truth until we are all miraculously transformed into an imperishable Spirit when we are redeemed by the Son of GOD.

Chapter 15: Unify with our God the Father and our Lord Jesus Christ

John 17:13-26 NIV

13 "I am coming to You now, but I say these things while I am still in the World, so that they may have the full measure of My joy within them.

14 I have given them Your Word and the World has hated them, for they are not of the World any more than I am of the World.

15 My prayer is not that You take them out of the World but that You protect them from the evil one.

16 They are not of the World, even as I am not of it.

17 Sanctify them by the Truth; Your Word is Truth.

18 As You sent Me into the World, I have sent them into the World.

19 For them I sanctify Myself, that they too may be truly sanctified."

20 "My prayer is not for them alone. I pray also for those who will believe in Me through their message,

21 that all of them may be One, Father, just as You are in Me and I am in You. May they also be in Us so that the World may believe that You have sent Me.

22 I have given them the glory that You gave Me, that they may be One as WE are One—

23 I in them and You in Me— So that they may be brought to complete unity. Then the World will know that You sent Me and have loved them even as You have loved Me.

24 "Father, I want those You have given Me to be with Me where I am, and to see My glory, the glory You have given Me because

You loved Me before the creation of the World.

25 Righteous Father, though the World does not know You, I know You, and they know that You have sent Me.

26 I have made You known to them and will continue to make You known in order that the love You have for Me may be in them and that I Myself may be in them.

❖ Notice:

Our Lord Jesus Christ prayed to our GOD the Father and asked HIM to protect us from the evil one because all protection against the evil one comes from the power in the NAME given by our GOD the Father. And our Lord Jesus Christ also asked HIM, for all believers to be in complete unity with THEM, including all those believing in the written message of the Word, that is in the Gospel, written as a Testimony for us by the Apostles that is now written in our heart by the Holy Spirit within us.

They wrote letters to explain the Testimony of our GOD the Father concerning HIS Son, who is our Lord Jesus Christ. First for people to learn and believe and then to have the Word from our GOD the Father sanctify their soul, heart, and mind, from the corruption of the World, to ready them for salvation by our Lord Jesus Christ with the Holy Spirit baptism in the NAME of Jesus Christ to cross over from death in the flesh, to live in the Spirit for eternal Life. It's now written and added within the New Testament of the Bible for all to learn and believe in THEM through the written message. That also includes us as believers living in the Spirit in this modern day and age. Because we are still living between the time of the resurrection of our Lord Jesus Christ and the appointed time of our redemption to enter eternal Life in the New Kingdom on the Last Day. This is the same day as the judgment Day is also reserved for the destruction of all the condemned because of the sins they Decided to remain living their lives in.

Chapter 15: Unify with our God the Father and our Lord Jesus Christ

The selfish are condemned because they are lovers of themselves and worldly things. They love the sin they commit and live with their sin in their flesh. Those who do not turn to believe in our Lord Jesus Christ are of this World. They keep their sin to live worldly and remain condemned and would rather reject to submitting and committing their personal Spirit through the NAME of our Lord Jesus Christ to be saved by the mercy of our GOD the Father with the eternal Life that HE put in HIS Son for us to have. No one goes to GOD the Father except through our Lord Jesus Christ the Son of our GOD the Father.

This Earth will pass away with Hades, with Sheol, with Death, and the condemned will pass away with them. But those living in Spirit now, will each be transformed into an imperishable Spirit Body for living in the New World Kingdom with our GOD the Father in complete unity. And HE will be our GOD living with us in the New Kingdom that HE will make for us.

Receiving, accepting, and believing this written message of the Word by the Apostle John, brings us into complete unity by our Decision to accept our Lord Jesus Christ to be living in us, and also accepting the Holy Spirit of our GOD the Father that we are baptized with to be living in us, at the moment that we believed it in our Heart, our Soul, and our Mind. And by that, we have decided to do what it says to do. From the moment that you are baptized in the NAME of our Lord Jesus Christ, you will receive the Seal of our GOD the Father, HIS Holy Spirit into you, and you become One with THEM forever. That's living in complete unity with THEM. The better you get at paying attention to what the Holy Spirit is guiding you to do, the more abundantly blessed you and the ones you love will be by our GOD the Father through our Lord Jesus Christ.

This is the Word, and it is the Truth.

- 1 John 5:10-12 (NIV)
    10 Whoever believes in the Son of GOD accepts this Testimony.

INSPIRATION FOR YOUR ETERNAL LIFE

> *Whoever does not believe GOD has made HIM out to be a liar, because they have not believed the Testimony GOD has given about HIS Son.* ***11** And this is the Testimony: **GOD has given us eternal Life, and this Life is in HIS Son**. **12** **Whoever has the Son has Life; whoever does not have the Son of GOD does not have Life.***

- **John 5:39-40 (NIV)**

  39 You study the scriptures diligently because you think that in them you have eternal Life. These are the very scriptures that Testify about Me, (Jesus Christ) *40 yet you refuse to come to Me to have Life.*

This is the New Covenant of our GOD the Father. For all who believe in HIM and have our Lord Jesus Christ in themselves will have eternal Life.

No one will ever be saved by only knowing what the scriptures say. That is like someone saying that that they believe in GOD because they know what the bible says, which is a lie and they don't realize what they are saying, and they are not saved living by that belief. You must first understand the Word of Truth and believe the Testimony of Our God the Father by contemplating on HIS Word of Truth and submitting and committing your personal Spirit to HIM in the NAME of HIS Son Jesus Christ, then live by HIS commands every day of your Life in complete unity with THEM. Everyone starts out that way until they accept the Truth in the Testimony of our GOD the Father about our Lord Jesus Christ. If you want to know if you are saved by the Grace of our GOD, the FATHER you can answer that question yourself. Ask yourself these questions:

- Do you contemplate on HIS Word of Truth every day by giving thanks to HIM while praying in Spirit to HIM in the NAME of HIS Son Jesus Christ? Yes.

Chapter 15: Unify with our God the Father and our Lord Jesus Christ

- Do you know the Testimony of our GOD the Father concerning HIS Son and the commands of our Lord Jesus Christ by heart? Yes.

- Do you know how to pray to our GOD the Father the way our Lord Jesus taught us to pray and what prerequisites are required by you to do before your prayers will be heard by our GOD the Father? Yes.

- Do you know how our GOD the FATHER wants us to ask of HIM to receive HIS Holy Spirit to be baptized? Yes.

- Do you know what believing in GOD means and how to live your life that way? Yes.

- Do you know, without a doubt, how you were saved to have eternal Life now and can prove it? Yes.

- Do you know the difference between the Old Covenant and the New Covenant? Yes.

- Do you know the New Command? Yes.

Those are some of the questions with the answers that you should know and answer yes to, to help you know without a doubt that you believe in our GOD the Father and that you are saved by HIS grace. If you cannot honestly answer yes to all those questions, then keep learning and practicing what you know until you can understand all the Truth in the Word and your faith will become impassible by doubt from the lies of the World.

The living power of the Life in our Lord Jesus Christ is our eternal Life in us. So, we must have our Lord Jesus Christ living in us, as we are made Holy by His authority and accept His help to give us eternal Life by the mercy of our GOD the Father allowing us to have the Right to become Holy Children of our GOD the Father through the authority given to our Lord Jesus Christ to forgive us of our sin. Even the evil ones that are demons that follow Satan, know what is written in the Bible. They were there when it happened, and they have rejected the Word of our GOD the Father. They were cast down here to Earth from Heaven before the Bible was written in stone and ink. And they know more about the past than Mankind has the need to know for the salvation of Mankind. Because we do not need to know anything else to be saved, except to believe in the Testimony of our GOD the Father by accepting it into our Heart to be justified and declaring with our Mouth that our Lord is Jesus Christ, the Son of our GOD the Father, then we can be saved.

We belong to our GOD the Father and our Lord Jesus Christ living in us in complete unity. We are One with THEM now as believers eternal Life has been put in our Mortal Body. You must embrace the Word and glorify our GOD the Father to have HIS Son, our Lord Jesus Christ, with the eternal Life in Him to be living in you and giving you eternal Life.

Every day that you wake up from your sleep, remember who you are, and that you have THEM living in you; as you live by your personal Spirit being guided by the Holy Spirit with THEM in you as One. By living in the Spirit now, you will learn to know our GOD the Father and to know our Lord Jesus Christ, and to know the Holy Spirit, then you will know what it really is to be in complete unity, with THEM in you. They will teach you to know THEM every day and moment of your Life. And because you have already crossed over from death to eternal life without sin with THEM, THEY will continue to Work with your Spirit to keep you Holy in learning the Word of Truth. They will Inspire your heart with true love that will fill your Body-Temple completely. You are completely Holy with THEM in you now, if you surely believe without doubt. And this is what you are fighting for to protect by praying in Spirit to our GOD the Father, in the NAME of our Lord Jesus Christ.

Keep the Word of Truth fresh in your Mind, Heart, and Soul, while doing the deeds that help yourself and others to reconcile with our GOD the Father, through our Lord Jesus Christ in Holiness and peace. The Angels in Heaven and the Children of GOD the Father on Earth rejoice every time someone turns to our Lord Jesus Christ to live in Spirit with the Holy Spirit as One. The Holy Spirit of our GOD the Father will be with you now and forever, and He will be told by our Lord Jesus Christ to

Chapter 15: Unify with our God the Father and our Lord Jesus Christ

raise you up at your appointed time, not to see judgment or shame, but to see redemption because you are made Holy when you are forgiven of your sins by the authority in our Lord Jesus Christ. And so, you will appear with Him in Holiness with the Holy Spirit to receive His love when you see Him in His glory on His Throne. He will call you to Himself to give you your redemption reward, as THEY promised you will receive the Crown Of Righteousness, Life, and Glory, for Deciding to live with THEM in complete unity. Then you will enter the New Kingdom of our GOD the Father, where HE will live among us forever.

This is the Word, and it is the Truth.

- ## 2 Corinthians 1:21-22 (NIV)
    21 Now it is GOD who makes both us and you stand firm in Christ. HE anointed us, 22 set HIS Seal of ownership on us, and put HIS Spirit in our hearts as a deposit, (Holy Spirit) guaranteeing what is to come.

The Holy Spirit is your guide to follow and to live in Holiness with. You are being kept protected from evil ones to remain Holy in Spirit for our Lord Jesus Christ and hidden in the power of our GOD the Father. You are being kept away from sin and evil ones, to avoid the appointed time for them; that is the reckoning on the judgment Day being reserved for the destruction of all the condemned.

Stay away from condemnation with the ones that do evil because they reject to believe in our Lord Jesus Christ. They reject the Testimony of our GOD the Father, and they do not keep the commands of our Lord Jesus Christ. They will be Judged by our Lord Jesus Christ, because of their own Decision to stay living in sin and to remain condemned. Their sinful and condemned Spirit will be raised to the judgment Seat to die a Second Death. That is not the First Death of the flesh, it is the Second Death of the Spirit, which is the complete destruction of their Spirit for not believing in our Lord Jesus Christ or the Testimony of our GOD the

Father who sent Him. They Decided not to receive His Holy Spirit of eternal Life and by that Decision that leads to condemnation, execution, and destruction of their personal Spirit.

Only our Lord Jesus Christ has been given the authority to give eternal Life and to judge condemnation and execute the destruction of anyone that is not One with Him, to destroy the existence and memory of all condemnation. Those that refuse our Lord Jesus Christ, have condemnation already and accept condemnation, stand for condemnation, and are helping others have condemnation, therefore they are condemnation without our Lord Jesus Christ. Those that accept our Lord Jesus Christ, have Life already and accept Life, stand for Life, and are helping others have Life, therefore they are Life with our Lord Jesus Christ.

On the Last Day, our Lord Jesus Christ will call both to rise up to His Throne in Heaven. Those that have Life will rise up to be redeemed and rewarded to receive the Crown of Life and live with the Right to enter The New Kingdom of GOD, on the New Earth with the New Heaven for eternal Life with HIM. Those who have condemnation will rise up into judgment to be destroyed by the Second Death, which is the death of their Spirit. Therefore, all condemnation will be destroyed.

The Earth and Death will be destroyed in the same way and place as all those that are condemnation will be consigned to and destroyed by fire. Since the Earth will be no more and Death is destroyed there will be no more condemnation or the memory of it. And the World will know that our GOD the Father has glorified HIS Son, our Lord Jesus Christ, and has Granted His Son the Authority to Judge over all things in Heaven and Earth to reconcile all things to HIMSELF, our GOD the Father.

- **John 5:26-29 (NIV)**
    26 For as the Father has Life in HIMSELF, so HE has granted the Son also to have Life in Himself. 27 And HE has

given Him Authority to Judge because He is the Son of Man. 28 "Do not be amazed at this, for a time is coming when all who are in their graves will hear His Voice 29 and come out—those who have done what is good will rise to Live, and those who have done what is evil will rise to be condemned.

- ### Revelation 21:8 (NIV)

    *8 But the Cowardly, the Unbelieving, the Vile, the Murderers, the Sexually Immoral, those who Practice Magic Arts, the Idolaters, and all Liars—They will be consigned to the **Fiery Lake** of burning sulfur. **This is the Second Death**."*

The Second Death is the final destination and final act of execution for the non-believers; they will be consigned to their final destination to be disposed of by their final doom and destruction of their Spirit. That is judgment and shame for their Decision not to live Holy in complete unity with our Lord Jesus Christ on Earth.

Our Lord Jesus Christ loves you and has His eternal Life in you, because of your pure heart that believes in Him, and the Words from your Mouth that you proclaim to all the World that our Lord is Jesus Christ, and He is your Lord. It is the will of our GOD the Father for everyone that HE calls to have eternal Life, and it is the will of our Lord Jesus Christ to do HIS will, to raise everyone that is called to eternal Life by our GOD the Father that accepts living by HIS righteousness in HIS New Covenant with us.

This is the Word, and it is the Truth.

- ### Romans 10:17 (NIV)

    17 Consequently, faith comes from hearing the message, and the message is heard through the word about Christ.

Praise our GOD the Father in the NAME of our Lord Jesus Christ that you are now sanctified and baptized with the Holy Spirit and working to keep the commands. You heard about and read the message in the Word, and we have learned it from the Gospel of the Apostle John. You are now sanctified by your faith in believing it and by believing the Truth, the message we learn from the Word passed down to us from our GOD the Father through our Lord Jesus Christ and written in the New Testament by the Apostle John that we believe in, that is Truth.

You must believe the Gospel about our Lord Jesus Christ, and the Testimony of our GOD the Father, by living and doing what the Word says to do. Living with the Holy Spirit and the Spirit of our Lord Jesus Christ in you now is to be already saved with the promise from our GOD the Father to redeem everyone who has HIS Son Jesus Christ our Lord. Keep reading and learning the Word by heart, and your faith will be as strong as the Truth you know, live by it, learn from it, and you will have eternal Life.

- **Ephesians 1:13-14 (NIV)**
    13 And you also were included in Christ when you heard the message of Truth, the Gospel of your salvation. When you believed, you were marked in Him with a Seal, the promised Holy Spirit, 14 who is a deposit guaranteeing our inheritance until the redemption of those who are GOD'S possession— **To the Praise of HIS Glory**.

Rest assured that our Lord Jesus Christ only asked for things that glorify our GOD the Father. And those things were granted without delay and without a doubt. We must do the same and have no doubt to receive what we ask for, in order to glorify our GOD the Father. Our Lord Jesus Christ asked for the Holy Spirit to be sent thousands of years ago. It was done then and is being done now. This is the appointed time that we are to live Holy in complete unity, to prove our trust and faith to THEM by living

Chapter 15: Unify with our God the Father and our Lord Jesus Christ

with THEM now. It is truly miraculous to have HIS Holy Spirit in our own hearts, working through us for the glory of our GOD the Father, in the NAME of HIS Son, Jesus Christ.

And our GOD the Father gives that which is everlasting because all things are possible only with the power of our GOD the Father. And HE gives us eternal Life through HIS Son, our Lord Jesus Christ. And since our Lord Jesus Christ has already returned to Heaven to be glorified again, He is sitting at the Right Hand of our GOD the Father, atoning for our weakness that we repent our sins for our own need for forgiveness.

- **Mathew 10:32 NIV)**
  32 "Whoever acknowledges Me before others, I will also acknowledge before My Father in Heaven, but whoever disowns Me before others, I will disown before My Father in Heaven.

- **Ephesians 1:18-23 (NIV)**
  18 I pray that the eyes of your heart may be enlightened in order that you may know the hope to which HE has called you, the riches of HIS glorious inheritance in HIS Holy people, 19 and HIS incomparably great power for us who believe. That power is the same as the mighty strength (GOD the Father) *20 HE exerted when HE raised Christ from the dead and seated Him at HIS Right Hand in the Heavenly Realms, 21 far above all rule and authority, power and dominion, and every Name that is invoked, not only in the present age but also in the one to come. 22 And GOD placed all things under His feet and appointed Him to be Head Over Everything for the Church, 23 which is His Body, the fullness of Him who fills everything in every way.*

Now you are sanctified and protected by the only true living GOD the Father; because you believe the Word, and the message in the Gospel written in the Testimony of the Apostle John, about our Lord Jesus Christ being sent from our GOD the Father to save us and reconcile us back to HIMSELF because HE loves us. The Body of our Lord Jesus Christ is the Church, and we are living in Him every moment of our lives.

These writings from the Apostle John, Chapters 13 through 17, give us the message in the Word, and the Gospel about our Lord Jesus Christ, who was sent by our GOD the Father to reconcile us and all creation back to HIMSELF. With this blessing, you already believe and have crossed over from death to eternal Life. And our Lord Jesus Christ has sent you the Seal, the Holy Spirit, that marks you in our Lord Jesus Christ and as a Child of GOD the Father. That is HIS guarantee to grant us eternal Life in the New Kingdom when all believers are redeemed on the Last Day when we are called up to live with our Lord Jesus Christ. We are now One, in complete unity with our Lord Jesus Christ and the Holy Spirit living in us. Be as fearless as our Lord Jesus Christ living in you, He has conquered all evil, sin, and death to save us.

- **Romans 8 (NIV)**
    11 And if the Spirit (Holy Spirit) of HIM (GOD the Father) *who raised Jesus from the dead is living in you, HE* (GOD the Father) *who raised Christ from the dead will also give Life to your Mortal Bodies because of HIS Spirit* (Holy Spirit) *who lives in you.*

Inspiration for your eternal Life comes from the power of our GOD the Father through HIS Son, our Lord Jesus Christ and the miracles of HIS Holy Spirit, who are all actively living within you now in complete unity.

Our GOD the Father has given us HIS mercy as a Holy gift for us to have

Chapter 15: Unify with our God the Father and our Lord Jesus Christ

eternal Life in the New Covenant of the Spirit and it is expressed in HIS Testimony about HIS Son, our Lord Jesus Christ. And our Lord Jesus Christ has given us HIS commands to have and obey so we may live with the likeness of His nature in His image. He has given us a New Command, which is a key message telling us how to live in the Spirit. Only those with this message written in their heart may enter the New Kingdom of Heaven. Our Lord Jesus Christ has given us this message for us to keep written in our hearts by the Holy Spirit, for each other to know for ourselves that we have eternal Life now. His key message that we must have within us is to "Always Love Each Other."

And this is our prayer:

We pray in Spirit to ask You, our GOD the Father, to help us remain in complete unity with You and our Lord Jesus Christ for eternal Life. We love Your Son, our Lord Jesus Christ. We hope to see Him with You in the glory He had in Heaven before the creation of the World.

We give thanks that You sent Your Son to teach us Your Word of Truth to know You, our GOD the Father, and Your Son, Jesus Christ. We ask that You keep us protected in the NAME of our Lord Jesus Christ, so we may see the day when He will raise us up to appear Holy in Your presence, so we may glorify You with our loved ones forever.

We pray to ask You in the NAME of Your Son, our Lord Jesus Christ.

INSPIRATION FOR YOUR ETERNAL LIFE

These letters are gifts of love being shared by people who pray for each other to help us remain attached to our Lord Jesus Christ every day. Someone you know may be hoping to find help to understand the Truth in the Bible to know our GOD the Father and turn to HIS Son our Lord Jesus Christ for eternal salvation.

Live in Spirit to stay Holy and contemplate on things in Heaven where our Lord Jesus Christ is. Share the Word to keep His commands every day until He raises you up Holy to appear with Him in Heaven to the glory of our GOD the Father who loves you and gives you the Inspiration for your eternal Life. Our Lord Jesus Christ is the Way, the Truth, and the Life.

This is the Word of GOD our Father concerning HIS Son Jesus Christ, and it is the Truth.

About the Author

Vincente R. Garcia was born November 1961 in Pontiac Michigan and raised in Southern California. About the age of seven, he had several spiritual interventions that would set the tone throughout his life. By the age of nine, he would put on a suit and walk alone to the local churches in Torrance California to join in singing and praising God in the early Sunday services.

From those early years, he felt a strong connection with the Spirit of our Lord Jesus Christ and knew that he was being called to know Him throughout his life. His focus was to venture on a quest to understand the messages he was shown by searching the Bibles the KJV, NIV, NWT, Gideon, and the Quran, mostly to learn the reason why spirits intervene with humanity and more with some than others.

After high school, he served in the United States Air Force Europe, then served in civil law enforcement in the California Department of Corrections during which time he also became an Ordained Minister by the Universal Life Church Ministries in June 2022. Shortly after, in February 2023 he was given a sign that it was time to Minister to the Lord. Without delay, in March 2023 he retired from employment and was immediately guided into powerful Spiritual Prayers for over 12 months, day and night, to write these fifteen letters as a foundation of truth for the children in the world who are being called to the living God. These letters are the results of his mission for the chosen ones, to help them understand how to become inspired for eternal life.

www.ingramcontent.com/pod-product-compliance
Lightning Source LLC
Chambersburg PA
CBHW082116230426
43671CB00015B/2715